P9-DVO-943

TALES & TRAILS

CALGARY PUBLIC LIBRARY

JUN ׀ ׀ 2011

TALES &
TRAILS

ADVENTURES
FOR EVERYONE IN THE
CANADIAN ROCKIES

LYNN MARTEL

RMB
Victoria Vancouver Calgary

Copyright © 2011 Lynn Martel

All rights reserved. No part of this publication may be reproduced, stored in a retrieval system, or transmitted in any form or by any means—electronic, mechanical, audio recording, or otherwise—without the written permission of the publisher or a photocopying licence from Access Copyright, Toronto, Canada.

Rocky Mountain Books
www.rmbooks.com

Library and Archives Canada Cataloguing in Publication

Martel, Lynn
    Tales and trails : adventures for everyone in the Canadian Rockies / by Lynn Martel.

Includes bibliographical references and index.
Issued also in an electronic format.
ISBN 978-1-926855-27-1

    1. Rocky Mountains, Canadian (B.C. and Alta.)—Description and travel.
2. Rocky Mountains, Canadian (B.C. and Alta.)—History. 3. Rocky Mountains, Canadian (B.C. and Alta.)—Guidebooks. I. Title.

FC219.M36 2011   971.23'32   C2011-900280-9

All photos by Lynn Martel, except:
cover photo: Paul Žižka, *All Shades Of Blue*, www.zizka.ca
p. 30: Olivia Sofer
p. 35, 183: Lynn Martel collection
p. 89, 180: Chic Scott
p. 132: Gail Crowe-Swords

Printed in Canada

Rocky Mountain Books acknowledges the financial support for its publishing program from the Government of Canada through the Canada Book Fund (CBF) and the province of British Columbia through the British Columbia Arts Council and the Book Publishing Tax Credit.

This book was produced using FSC®-certified, acid-free paper, processed chlorine free and printed with vegetable-based inks.

Disclaimer

The actions described in this book may be considered inherently dangerous activities. Individuals undertake these activities at their own risk. The information put forth in this guide has been collected from a variety of sources and is not guaranteed to be completely accurate or reliable. Many conditions and some information may change owing to weather and numerous other factors beyond the control of the author and publisher. Individual climbers and/or hikers must determine the risks, use their own judgment, and take full responsibility for their actions. Do not depend on any information found in this book for your own personal safety. Your safety depends on your own good judgment based on your skills, education, and experience.

    It is up to the users of this guidebook to acquire the necessary skills for safe experiences and to exercise caution in potentially hazardous areas. The author and publisher of this guide accept no responsibility for your actions or the results that occur from another's actions, choices, or judgments. If you have any doubt as to your safety or your ability to attempt anything described in this guidebook, do not attempt it.

Contents

Welcome to My World

I arrived in the Canadian Rockies in the same timeless way so many young people do. In 1982, my sister, Daisy, who was just nineteen, followed her already well-developed travel instincts to Banff from our hometown of Montreal, Quebec, on the eastern side of this vast country. I can still remember her first phone call home and her excited voice describing "mountains everywhere!"

Within a few months I flew out to visit her and visited again several months later. In the spring of 1984, as soon as my semester at Concordia University, where I was studying creative writing, was over, I headed straight for Banff for my fifth visit, thinking if I scored a job I'd stay the summer.

I've never lived in Montreal since, and other than a few brief stints in Ontario, Maui and Whistler, I've made the Bow Valley – first Banff, and since 2000, Canmore – home.

While I was hopelessly drawn to the obvious beauty and spectacular physical presence of the mountains, like so many young Banff workers I spent a lot more of my first eighteen months in the Rockies frequenting the Banff Avenue nightlife scene than I did the mountain trails. By summer 1986, however, I could no longer ignore my need to explore beyond the pavement. Somehow I scraped together enough of my minimum-wage earnings in retail to purchase a mountain bike, at that time still an exciting new recreation technology.

Starting with short rides to the Cave and Basin or Vermilion Lakes Drive, I began to explore my mountain home. Before long my confidence and my physical strength grew, as did the distances I pedalled. Over the years, that confidence and curiosity spilled over to other mountain sports – backpacking, snowboarding, then backcountry ski touring, rock climbing and mountaineering.

Eventually, I began to share my adventures – the lessons I learned from being tired and sore and cold, and the stories of our unique mountain history and culture and the fascinating people who have made their own mark on these mountains – through writing for newspapers and magazines.

For me, participating in these activities has always been more about exploring the wilderness landscape than any pursuit of a fleeting adrenaline rush. Rather, I am lured by the peace I find in the mountains.

Spending hours and days in the backcountry, waking up in tents and simple huts and hiking and skiing up valleys and over passes and across glaciers have taught me how every living organism on this planet is interconnected, and that without a healthy Mother Earth, nothing can survive.

They've taught me to appreciate every breath I am blessed to take, every adventure I am grateful to experience, and every friendship I'm so fortunate to share.

These mountains have taught me my place in this world. Welcome to my world, the Canadian Rockies.

—Lynn Martel
Canmore, Alberta
March 2011

Life is Short!

Take a Hike and Smell the Alpine Wildflowers

There's no mystery to outdoor adventure or backcountry travel. It's like everything else: start at the beginning, like riding a bike, driving a car or playing the accordion. Learn the basics, be patient, have fun and repeat often. The more often you walk, ski or ride your bike uphill, the easier it will become – and the smaller your backside! Take lessons; join outdoor clubs such as the Alpine Club of Canada or your local canoe club to meet experienced partners. Learn what can hurt you (or worse) and how best to avoid those things. Take a basic first aid course so you'll know how to handle an emergency if you start venturing more than a half-hour from your car. Remember, though, driving a car or slipping in the bathtub injures more people every day than hiking or climbing do. Pick an activity that's right for you. If you don't like or are afraid of water, kayaking is probably not a good choice. That is, unless you're the type of personality that thrives on overcoming your fears, in which case, well, you should just give 'er!

The trips listed in this book represent a very small sampling – barely a nibble – of the countless opportunities for all sorts of backcountry experiences available in the Canadian Rockies. Hopefully the stories and the trip suggestions will only whet your appetite for many, many more adventures! You'll find an extensive list of comprehensive regional guidebooks and reference books on page 204.

TRIP RATINGS

Family Friendly The average person can walk at a pace of about 4 kilometres per hour, give or take. These trips average 4 to 6 kilometres round-trip (two to three hours at a relaxed pace), and are suitable for all levels of fitness and leg length!

They involve clearly marked, well-graded trails with minimal elevation gain and no technical challenges, and require only a small daypack. Never worry if you don't reach your "destination," the adventure is in the journey, not any arbitrary end point. For extra fun, pack a bird or flower identification book.

Sweat a Little These adventures are suitable for any moderately fit person who is prepared to walk, cycle or cross-country ski for four to six hours. They involve carrying a daypack or single-night backpack on trails that are clearly marked, well-travelled trails with moderate uphill and short sections of steeper or rugged terrain. Some involve easy scrambling where a helmet is recommended but no technical skills are needed.

Sweat a Lot These adventures will appeal to those with a fair bit of experience who are reasonably fit and strong and most importantly, eager and willing to hike or ski for six to ten hours at a time. They often involve carrying a backpack on trails that are frequently rugged, though usually well-travelled, and which might involve uphill walking for extended periods of time. Any trip involving technical terrain, such as rock climbing or glacier travel, should only be undertaken by those who have taken courses taught by professional instructors, or in the company of a professional guide.

Bust a Lung! Why settle for double black diamond when you can triple your fun? These adventures are for the extremely fit who possess extensive backcountry experience. They often involve carrying multi-day backpacks weighing at least 20 kilograms (40 pounds), including ropes, harnesses, glacier and technical climbing equipment, plus shovels, probes and transceivers for backcountry skiing. These trips involve travelling off-trail over rugged and often unmarked wilderness terrain hours or days from the nearest trailhead, and days can last upwards of 12 hours each. Anyone who feels fit enough for such adventures but lacks the crucial route-finding, technical and decision-making skills and experience to undertake such a trip safely and self-sufficiently, should hire a professional guide for the adventure of a lifetime!

ACTIVITY TYPES

Kayaking/whitewater rafting

Mountaineering/climbing

Ice climbing

Backcountry ski touring

Cross-country skiing

Hiking

Backpacking

Mountain biking

Horseback riding

Caving

Camping

Climbers hut

Lodge/deluxe hut

TAKE A LESSON OR HIRE A GUIDE

You don't have to be trying to climb Mount Robson to appreciate the expertise of a professional guide, so if you're new to the mountain wilderness or unsure about your abilities or confidence, hire a hiking guide for a day or even your first backpacking adventure. Not only will they keep you safe, but an experienced guide will happily share a backpack's worth of knowledge about the plants and animals and geology of the Rockies landscape – and give you tips about how to avoid getting blisters:
www.banfftours.com
www.whitemountainadventures.com
www.naturalhighalpine.com

www.greatdivide.ca
www.overlandertrekking.com

Don't even think about rock climbing, mountaineering, backcountry ski touring in avalanche terrain, ice climbing or stepping one foot on a glacier without hiring a professional guide, or before taking a course taught by a professional guide certified through the Association of Canadian Mountain Guides. Don't attempt kayaking without professional lessons either. To hire a guide or to sign up for a mountain skills course from beginner to advanced, check out the following:

www.acmg.ca
www.yamnuska.com
www.internationalguidebureau.com
www.alpineclubofcanada.ca

To locate a paddling guide in your area, visit www.out-there.com.

WEATHER

Among locals, Canadian Rockies weather is considered a legitimate, often fascinating, and from time to time, exasperating topic of conversation. During the winter, warm winds known regionally as Chinooks can cause the temperature to rise 20 degrees over three hours. Naturally, drops can be quick and severe too. My first winter camping experience happened on the Skyline hiking trail in Jasper in the middle of August. The saying "if you don't like the weather, wait five minutes" applies very accurately in these mountains. If dressing in layers wasn't invented in the Rockies, it should have been. Check the forecast before heading out, but always be prepared for it to change with little notice:

www.weatheroffice.gc.ca
www.theweathernetwork.com

No matter the season, never travel more than 30 minutes from your car in the Canadian Rockies without:

- basic first aid kit
- sunglasses and sunscreen

- toque and/or sun hat
- gloves
- warm layer
- waterproof, wind-resistant layer
- water and snacks
- matches or lighter
- map and compass
- bear spray (in summer)
- camera!

BEARS, WOLVERINES, PIKAS AND OTHER WILD CRITTERS

The Canadian Rockies are home to a myriad of wild creatures, from grizzly bears to bighorn sheep to pine martens to voles. Their presence is one of the things that makes wilderness travel so very special and so interesting. Before you set out, take the time to learn how to be a safe, responsible backcountry traveller by visiting any of the Kananaskis Country or Parks Canada visitor information centres, or at www.tpr.alberta.ca/parks/kananaskis and www.parksmountainsafety.ca.

National parks, provincial parks and other protected areas have different rules regarding dogs, so make sure you know those rules before heading into the backcountry with your four-legged best friend. In most cases it's advisable to keep your dog on leash in the backcountry to avoid the unpleasant possibility of him enticing a much larger, faster-running critter to come and meet you.

Bear bells are silly, annoying and can only be heard by the person walking beside you. Do you really think a tinkling bell sounds like something a bear should run away from? Share conversation with your travelling companions, sing and shout occasionally to let the animals know a human is passing through. Give bears and all wild animals lots of room. The vast majority of the time they will leave the area before you figure out what you just heard or, if you're really lucky, saw.

Keep your eyes and ears open, and yes, leave that iPod at

home, too. Give your technologically overloaded senses a break. You wouldn't hike or mountain bike blindfolded to the dazzling mountain scenery, or with your nose pinched shut to the tangy scent of juniper, so why plug your ears to the music of a trickling creek, the captivating rat-a-tat of a prehistoric-looking pileated woodpecker or the musical rustlings of wind through the forest? Besides, the bears can hear you, so for safety's sake, you should be listening for them too.

CELL PHONES, PERSONAL TRACKING DEVICES AND OTHER SHINY GADGETS

If you do pack your cell or smart phone, BE AWARE: while it will work in some locations, there is no reliable cell phone coverage in most of the Canadian Rockies backcountry. A satellite phone costs more and weighs more, but works just about everywhere. A SPOT personal tracking device is also very useful, but does have some limitations that must be understood long before you need to use it.

A GPS too is a very useful device, but since batteries can die and electronic devices can fail, it's always advisable to carry a map and compass as a backup – with the knowledge of how to use them.

FOOTWEAR

Be nice to your feet – shop at a well-established outdoor retailer and buy sturdy footwear that fits well. Trail shoes are sufficient for easy to moderate trips, but if you're carrying a multi-day pack it's a good idea to wear boots with solid ankle support. Whether shopping for ski boots, rock shoes or mountaineering boots, women should try on female-specific models first. Always chose a good fit over your favourite colour. A muddy trail or really chossy rock will change that colour pretty quickly anyway.

BACKPACKS

Be nice to your back too, and it will be happy to carry your eyes, ears, mind and body around to fascinating places for a good many years. Just like with footwear, always shop at specialty outdoor shops. A good shop will have a few sandbags on hand to drop into the pack so you'll know how it will fit with some weight in it. Don't buy a pack bigger than you need – the bigger your pack, the more tempted you'll be to stuff way more than you need into it, and you'll be really sorry a third of the way to your destination. Smaller women should look for female-specific packs that fit well according to the length of their backs.

FUEL

Always chose high-energy food such as nuts, dates, beef jerky or peanut butter sandwiches on multi-grain bread for your mountain adventures. Chips and Ichiban might taste good but they won't provide much in the way of body fuel. Pay attention to your body and treat it well with a healthy diet. And always make room for a bite of good-quality chocolate, and on over-night trips a wee sip of single malt scotch!

TENTS, SKIS, CRAMPONS AND MORE

If you've taken the basic skills courses or gained the experience to use crampons and ice axes and ropes and backcountry skis, then when it's time to purchase your own gear keep in mind that with so much great equipment out there, surf the web and do your homework. Think about how you plan to use your gear, and look for gear that suits your style, your ability and your purpose. If your budget is limited, look for used gear on websites such as www.kijiji.ca or www.craigslist.ca or the gear swap at www.mec.ca.

MAPS, PERMITS AND COMMON SENSE ...

Most hiking trails in the mountain parks are well marked with signs at key junctions, but still it's a good idea—and great fun—to learn how to read a topographical map. To obtain the appropriate topographical maps for the area you plan to visit, check out http://atlas.nrcan.gc.ca or www.gemtrek.com.

Also, Mapitfirst software is easy and fun to use and can be

downloaded to your GPS before heading out (Windows only): www.mapitfirst.ca.

If you plan to camp in the backcountry of any of the mountain parks, you'll need to acquire a backcountry permit from the appropriate Parks Canada or Kananaskis Country information centre. You will also need to learn the rules of safe camping in bear country.

www.tpr.alberta.ca/parks/kananaskis

Banff: 403.762.1550

Lake Louise: 403.522.3833

Yoho (Field, BC) toll free at 1.866.787.6221, or 250.343.6783

Kootenay (Radium, BC): 250.347.9505

Jasper: 780.852.6176

Remember, if you're scrambling, always wear a helmet. On a glacier, always rope up. When you're backcountry skiing in avalanche terrain, never go anywhere without a shovel, probe, properly working transceiver and the knowledge of how to use these tools and perform a rescue. For avalanche conditions across western Canada, check the area you plan to visit at www.avalanche.ca.

DISCLAIMER

All backcountry adventures come with some degree of risk. It is the responsibility of the individual to become informed as to those risks, and to know how to deal with any emergency that might happen a dozen kilometres from the trailhead. If you are uncertain about your abilities or your level of confidence, hire a professional guide or take a skills course from professional instructors.

The author has made every attempt to be as accurate as possible with regard to distances on highways and trails and elevations of trailheads and mountaintops. While those numbers might be off by a fraction from time to time, if you're having fun enjoying the miraculous scenery and not obsessing about the accuracy of your shiny new electronic devices, your adventure should work out perfectly. If by chance you come across a really significant difference, I'd love to hear about it at lynnmartel@lynnmartel.ca.

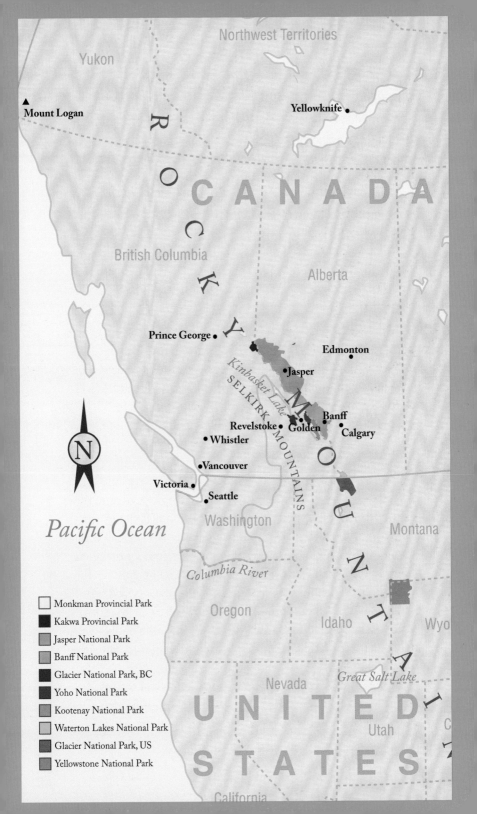

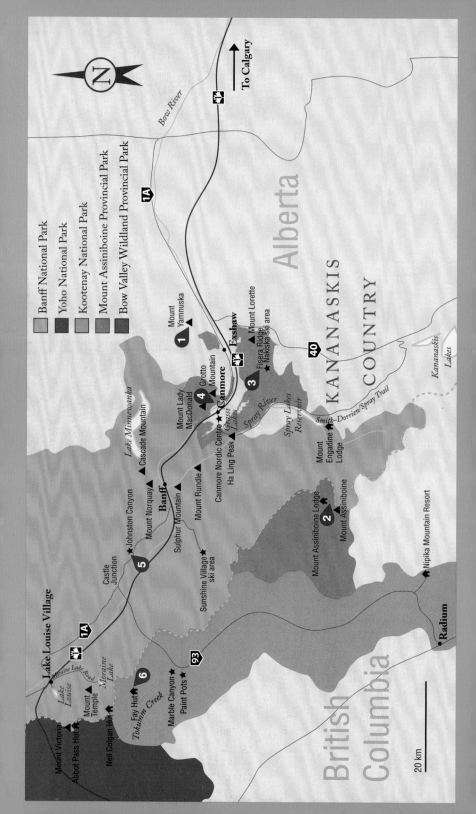

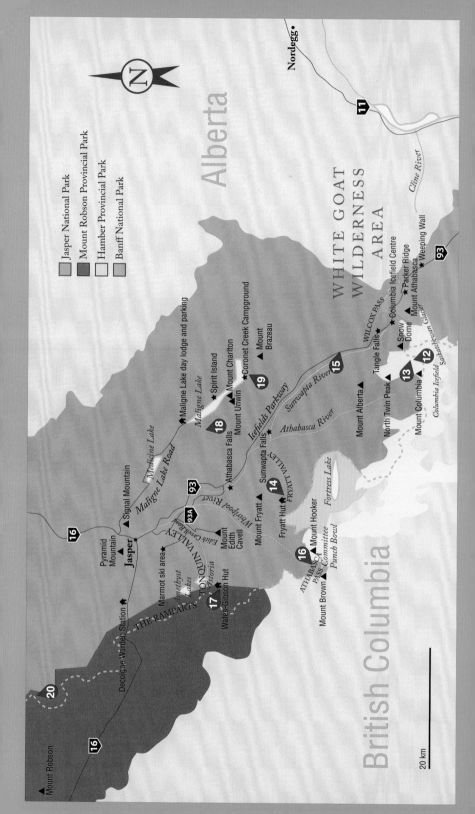

Canada's First Modern Climb

I n the annals of Canadian Rockies mountaineering history, the story is legend. On a warm November day in 1952, a group of climbers drove west from Calgary along the single-lane highway now known as the 1A. They parked at the base of Mount Yamnuska, the south-facing vertical wall of rock rising above the north bank of the Bow River at the eastern edge of the Rockies.

Among the group were Hans Gmoser and Leo Grillmair, two recent immigrants from Austria in their early twenties. Although both were experienced rock climbers, they had never shared a rope in their homeland. Gmoser had already been climbing several times in his newly adopted country, but Grillmair had been nursing a broken leg. Grillmair had now healed and he was extra keen to explore this new rock face, which resembled some cliffs they both had often climbed in Austria.

Wearing crepe-soled street shoes, Grillmair quickly scampered up the first cliff above the loose scree ledges at the mountain's base. Following on his rope was Isabel Spreat, an English physiotherapist who had been climbing at every opportunity since arriving in Canada two years earlier. Gmoser climbed with two others on a second rope, and two more climbed on a third. As the teams made their way up a series of corners and cracks, they realized they were moving too slowly and those below were in serious danger from rockfall dislodged by the climbers above them, so Gmoser soloed up to join Grillmair and Spreat while the others all descended.

After Grillmair led up a tricky step with small holds and very large exposure beneath him, he then belayed his rope-mates up. Having reached the base of a large chimney, the climbers peered up into the dark, vertical cave that penetrated deep inside the mountain face, wondering if they could find a route through. As snow began to fall from the late afternoon sky, Grillmair climbed upward into the chimney, dreading the thought of having to reverse the route and climb down rock that was now wet and slippery. Then, looking up, he noticed light streaming through the stone ceiling. Reaching it, he discovered a hole just large enough to fit his body through. Belaying his partners up, Grillmair was thrilled to have piloted a route on Yamnuska's steep south face, which they would christen Grillmair Chimneys.

While there is some evidence the route may have been climbed earlier by Lawrence Grassi, an Italian immigrant coal miner in Canmore who, when he died in 1980, left a legacy of extraordinary trail-building efforts, no formal record of his climb has been found. So Gmoser, Grillmair and Spreat, in making their ascent, had unknowingly established what would be considered the first modern climb in western Canada.

"It was huge," says Chic Scott, author of *Pushing the Limits*, an encyclopedic history of Canadian climbing. "In my opinion, the ascent of Grillmair Chimneys was the start of modern climbing in Canada. Up to that point, climbing in Canada was to get to the top of a mountain, and ideally make a first ascent. Grillmair Chimneys was the turning point – whether they got to the summit or not, the point was to climb a difficult route for the joy of climbing."

For Gmoser and Grillmair, the Grillmair Chimneys climb

was only the beginning. A year later, Gmoser, with Franz Dopf, another recent émigré from Austria who had been Gmoser's climbing partner in the old country, added a second route to Yamnuska, which they named the Calgary Route. In 1957, Gmoser, Grillmair, Dopf and two other Austrians, Kurt Lucas and Heinz Kahl, followed up with what would become another Yamnuska classic, Direttissima. For the remainder of that decade Yamnuska's cliffs were the solitary domain of only a handful of local climbers with the requisite skills, experience and boldness to ascend what some Stoney natives called the "flat-faced mountain."

"IS THIS REALLY 5.6?"

In July 2008, I set out with Robson Gmoser, the thirty-nine-year-old son of Hans Gmoser, and his fiancée, Olivia Sofer. None of us had climbed Grillmair Chimneys before; despite many years of Rockies climbing, it was my first route on the Yam.

Olivia Sofer, left, and Robson Gmoser walk along the base of Mount Yamnuska's south-facing wall on the approach to Grillmair Chimneys climbing route.

Olivia and Robson were both strong from nearly two dozen days of rock climbing that season, but I had only been out a handful of times. And while much of the climbing was easy clambering over giant blocks, ledges and steps, more than a few times during the five-hour ascent each of us commented on how the route seemed a lot more difficult than its "easy" 5.6 grade as we encountered tricky sections and awkward chimney moves.

And more than once we wondered how Grillmair and his partners might have felt climbing the 295-metre (968-foot) route without any idea of what the rock face had in store above them.

"This doesn't feel like 5.6," I muttered as I felt around on the rock above my ahead for a hold large enough to grab on to so I'd have the confidence to move my sticky-soled rock shoe onto a step the width of a toothbrush handle.

"Maybe you need to wear your street shoes," teased Robson as he belayed me from a table-sized ledge a few metres above, making reference to Grillmair's much less specialized first-ascent shoes. Robson led every pitch of our ascent, securing the rope to removable metal wedges and camming devices which he placed solidly in cracks as he proceeded, and which would prevent him from falling more than a few metres should he miss his footing or if a hold were to break. Once he had secured himself to a solid anchor point, Olivia and I followed safely, with Robson managing the rope from above and us removing the pieces of protection as we made our way upward.

Higher up the wall, I started up the final chimney, spanning my legs across the metre-wide gap, aware of the intimidating open space below me. Shifting my weight to the left wall, then the right, I moved up one foot and one hand at a time. The climbing was physical and sustained. Deep inside the chimney, the air was cool and I took off my sunglasses to see in the dark. Following the rope, I spied the hole. I removed my day pack and handed it up to Robson, and found the hole just large enough for me to fit through.

Robson Gmoser leads up the final chimney pitch of Grillmair Chimneys in July 2008, his first time climbing the route his father, Hans, put up with Leo Grillmair in 1952.

OLIVIA SOFER

LOCALS' LORE: *High, high up on a route called Unnamed, climbers are surprised to meet a giant orange pumpkin face painted on the wall. The creative graffiti is the handiwork of some Halloween pranksters equipped with a rope, paint and bubbly spirits in 1968.*

Laughing and covered in bumps, scrapes and bruises, I popped up through the hole to join Robson sitting comfortably among large boulders near the hiker's trail on Yamnuska's gently sloping back side, which would provide us an easy hike down.

"That was pretty staunch 5.6," Robson chuckled.

A week or so afterward, I spoke to Grillmair, who remembered his namesake climb well.

"We were in a snowstorm at the end," he described in his lyrical, frequently colourful and still thickly accented English. "I was leading, then Isabel, then Hans at the bottom. When we got to the bottom of the [final] chimney, I got a little worried. It didn't look too encouraging. I knew I could handle the chimney and I didn't want to go back down – it's not a good thing in a snowstorm when the rock gets all wet. My hands were getting cold and I was wearing only street shoes. I thought, I'll keep going up the chimney. All of a sudden I saw light, and I thought, Jesus, there's a hole up there! It was just big enough to fit my body through – I was only 130 pounds back then; I could go through it like a snake. By the time we got down to the bottom of the mountain, the soles of my shoes were coming off!"

Over the years, Grillmair said, he repeated the route many times.

"I climbed it a lot of times without a rope, by myself," Grillmair recalled. "I got to know the route quite well. Now I'm seventy-eight and I wouldn't want to do it now, not like that! At that time I had very strong arms. I was a plumber, and back then the pipes were galvanized steel and we screwed them together by hand before we used a pipe wrench. Do that a hundred times a day – my grip was so strong, my hands were incredible strong. I just put my arms across and pulled myself up. I could spread my legs and pull myself up with my knees. That was my specialty.

"When we came to Canada, Hans and I, the rock climbing wasn't done yet. The Alpine Club, they climbed the easy route to the summit. We looked for the hardest route up; the peak wasn't important. It looked like a nice face for good climbing. After that, Hans and I, we put some harder routes up, and then Brian Greenwood and those guys, they put up some really hard routes."

Today Yamnuska hosts more than 100 routes of widely ranging difficulty and climbing styles on its fractured limestone cliff face.

Hans Gmoser, meanwhile, with Grillmair at his side, became known worldwide for his bold and visionary climbing and ski touring expeditions, and for launching the helicopter skiing industry with his company, Canadian Mountain Holidays. In 1963 both Gmoser and Grillmair were instrumental in founding the Association of Canadian Mountain Guides (ACMG), which ten years later became the first non-European member of the International Federation of Mountain Guides Associations. Hans Gmoser received numerous awards and accolades, including the Order of Canada, before his untimely death as a result of a 2006 cycling accident.

For Robson Gmoser, an ACMG-certified ski guide and assistant rock guide (http://wildtrips.ca), climbing the route his father put up with Leo Grillmair more than a half-century earlier carried special meaning.

"I think it was quite neat to see what those guys had done. It makes you feel proud of your dad," Robson said. "It's quite an amazing climb, that they had the gumption to do it. I'm happy to have done it. I'm also trying to imagine them climbing through that little hole. It's a pretty neat thing, for the first route on Yam."

Robson said he didn't remember his dad talking about his climbs very much, particularly since Hans quit rock climbing after he was seriously injured by falling rock the same year Robson was born.

"I heard a few stories here and there, especially about Direttissima and using wooden pegs for protection," Robson recalled. "The only thing I remembered from Grillmair Chimneys is that they only used one piton."

Grillmair, however, adamantly denied having used any pitons on a route that most climbers today protect with at least several pieces of gear on each of its eight pitches.

"We didn't use pitons or anything like that," Grillmair said. "In those days, if we needed hardware, I wasn't interested. First of all, we didn't have it, but it wasn't my style. It's good Robson climbed it; it's easy for those young guys, the way they climb now. Robson's a good climber. Besides, it's not that difficult a route.

"I read an American magazine once that gave me credit for starting rock climbing in North America. I had no idea," he shrugged. "It's almost embarrassing."

Best seasons: As a south-facing mountain located at the lean end of the Rockies snowfall zone, Yamnuska can be enjoyed by hikers and even rock climbers year round. But the sprawling aspen forest at its base is simply jaw-dropping when the leaves turn gold in mid- to late September.

Trailhead: Park in a large gravel lot accessed from a short dirt road on the north side of Highway 1A at 2.1 kilometres (1.3 miles) east of the Highway 1X junction. Look for the trail sign at the north end of the parking lot. Follow the main hiking trail to a signed junction at the top of a short steep section. Topo map *Canmore 82 O/3*.

Family Friendly

Raven's End, 3.5 kilometres (2.2 miles) one-way, 520 metres (1,706 feet) elevation gain, high point 1890 metres (6,200 feet).

Raven's End is, you guessed it, a favourite hangout for the Rockies' most interesting and entertaining feathered inhabitants – not to mention the title of a delightful novel by Ben Gadd. Don't be deterred by the early steep bit; the trail eases off from there with only the occasional steep section. At the junction after the first steep section, take the right-hand hikers' route. It won't matter whether you reach the top or not; the views are fabulous long before you get there. Alternatively, head west into meadows right from the parking lot, where summer wildflowers bloom in rainbow splendour.

Scramble to the summit, 900 metres (2,953 feet) elevation gain, high point 2240 metres (7,349 feet). Helmet required.

From the junction take the left-hand option for a short distance and look for a smaller trail that branches off to the right. Follow it steeply uphill to where it intersects the hiking trail under the steep rock walls that form the far east end of the mountain. Put your helmet on here. Look for a trail that leads up into a small chimney feature and clamber up. It's a short section but fun. Beyond there, follow a well-travelled trail all the way to the summit. Hold on tight to the chains at that short section.

To descend, either retrace your steps or follow the trail down the northwest side of the mountain. It's a bit rougher than the east side, with plenty of slippery scree, but it allows you to complete the circuit by following the climbers' descent paths down a scree field under Yamnuska's giant south-facing cliff. Keep your helmet on until you're well into the trees.

Grillmair Chimneys. Although a technical rock climb, this can be accomplished by a strong, fit novice rock climber following a certified mountain guide.

If you're an experienced, competent rock climber, check out the full route description in *Bow Valley Rock*, by Chris Perry and Joe Josephson.

Test your tendons on Yamabushi, 300 metres (984 feet) eight pitches, 5.13a, put up by world-famous professional multi-sport athlete – and Canadian Rockies local – Will Gadd. Check out my all-time favourite homepage health warning at http://willgadd.com. For a route topo, go to http://tabvar.org.

Author Lynn Martel pops through the hole that marks the finish of Grillmair Chimneys, with Robson Gmoser belaying.

LYNN MARTEL COLLECTION

Hire a guide: If you don't have the requisite skills and experience, hire a guide to take you on any of these adventures or to organize a custom trip: www.acmg.ca, www.yamnuska.com or www.internationalguidebureau.com.

Trail ride: Settle into the saddle for a two-hour horseback ride along the banks of the Bow River at the Kananaskis Guest Ranch, run by the Brewster family, now in its sixth generation, the longest-running family-operated business in the Canadian Rockies. Or indulge a dream and join one of their overnight trips to a backcountry camp: http://kananaskisguestranch.com.

2

Skiing into History at Assiniboine

"Good mooorning!"

Outside our cozy, single-room log cabin, Sepp Renner's musical Swiss accent rang out like a chime in the crisp mountain air as he delivered a small bucket of warm water for us to wash the sleep from our eyes.

Hiking through newly fallen, shin-deep snow, my sister, Daisy, and I followed the aroma of fresh baking through the heavy wooden door into the dining room at Mount Assiniboine Lodge's main building a few minutes away. Our tummies filled, we listened as Sepp outlined the day's program to two dozen guests gathered around wooden tables. Sepp would lead a gentle cross-country ski tour across rolling hills and meadows, while his son André would indulge those eager for steeper climbs and powder turns.

We joined André's group.

With synthetic climbing skins applied to our ski bases, we climbed the slopes of Nub Peak, the group conversation ranging from the contents of our pack lunches to the "war on terror" to global warming and the Rockies' snowpack that year. Despite blizzard conditions above treeline, André led us to half a dozen untracked powder runs in sheltered forest, prompting Doug, skiing with his son Duncan, to exclaim at the bottom of each run, "That was FUN!"

Relaxing in the sauna before dinner, Simon, another lodge guest, mused, "We go out and sweat all day, then we go in the sauna and sweat some more."

Less than one hour's drive and only a nine-minute helicopter flight from Canmore's Main Street, I felt like I was in a distant, enchanted world.

Dinner was followed by storytelling, led by frequent Assiniboine guest Hans Gmoser, founder of the world's first helicopter skiing company, Canadian Mountain Holidays. Gmoser told tales of the Marquis Nicholas degli Albizzi, a Russian/Italian nobleman who first visited Assiniboine in 1927 by horseback in the company of Alpine Club of Canada founder A.O. Wheeler.

Once home, Albizzi, who was winter sports director at Lake Placid, New York, proposed an expedition to ski to Assiniboine to Norwegian ski pioneer Erling Strom. In March 1928, Strom and Albizzi arrived in Banff with four guests, only to discover that spring had arrived early in the Bow Valley.

Undeterred by snickering locals, including grizzled outfitter Tom Wilson, who declared, "There ought to be open season on people like you," Albizzi's party took two days to ski 50 kilometres (31 miles) from the Banff townsite to Assiniboine via Brewster Creek, overnighting at the Canadian Pacific Railway's cabin below Allenby Pass. Strom and Albizzi spent three more exhausting days ferrying supplies from the CPR cabin to Wheeler's Wonder Lodge, which is now known as Naiset Cabins, tucked in the meadows at the foot of the towering pyramid of Mount Assiniboine. Once settled in, the group was rewarded with seventeen sunny days to explore boundless skiing options.

Back in New York, Albizzi persuaded Canadian Pacific to build Assiniboine Lodge, promising to supply guests through his Lake Placid connections. With every shingle and pane of glass packed in on horseback, the main building and six cabins

Backcountry skiers in Mount Assiniboine Provincial Park ascend Ellie's Knob in anticipation of a long run down.

were built in 1928, making it the North American Rockies' first backcountry ski lodge. Strom ran the lodge for the next half century. In the mid-1930s, Brewster outfitters built Sunburst Cabin by Sunburst Lake, then sold it in 1950 to Lizzie Rummel. A German baroness who spent most of her adult life running lodges in the Canadian Rockies for backcountry visitors, Rummel hosted guests at Sunburst Cabin for twenty-five years. The public elementary school in Canmore and a lovely alpine lake in Kananaskis Country are named for Rummel, who died in 1980, in honour of her deep commitment to her adopted home in the Rockies.

Only three additions have been made to Assiniboine Lodge since its initial construction – the living room with upstairs bedrooms in 1963, a small pack house around 1950, and the log-cabin sauna, including two showers, in 1996. Apart from propane heat and lanterns and thrice-weekly helicopter shuttles, little has changed since. Guests arrive from places such as

Rhode Island, New York, New Jersey, Vancouver and Calgary, some opting to ski or, in summer, hike all the way in amidst a landscape of soaring peaks, splashing creeks and sparkling turquoise lakes. The shortest route is 28 kilometres (17 miles) from Kananaskis Country's Mount Shark trailhead.

Upstairs in the lodge, delicate lace curtains frame bedroom windows from where one might marvel at the sunrise casting an ethereal glow on Mount Assiniboine's dramatic, chiselled summit. The living room is furnished with log-frame couches and roadkill elkhide armchairs arranged around a coal-fired stove. In the dining room, walls display wooden skis that belonged to one of the lodge's very first guests. A painted Norwegian dragon frames the names of the first decade's skiers engraved in the log beams. Black and white photos honour Rummel, Strom, Banff packer Al Johnson, and Ken Jones, who was Mount Assiniboine Provincial Park's first ranger. Jones, who died in 2004, had continued to lead hikers on trails around Assiniboine until his nineties. He was also the first Canadian to earn his mountain guide's certification, in 1933, trained by the Swiss guides who established the Rockies' professional guiding tradition in the early 1900s. One photo dated 1953 shows Rummel listening intently to a young Hans Gmoser and his climbing partner Franz Dopf describing their climb of Mount Assiniboine.

It was earlier in 1952 that by chance Gmoser had first met Jones and Rummel as they dried their climbing skins in a Banff backyard after skiing from Assiniboine. The encounter yielded the young Austrian his first Canadian guiding work – helping Rummel and Strom with their guests for two winters.

"One of the most fantastic things about the job was being able to – having to – ski from Assiniboine to Sunshine to pick up guests," Gmoser recalled after dinner.

Usually an eight- to ten-hour ski one way, he described how on one day he had struggled to break trail through deep, heavy snow as he led his charges on the 29-kilometre (18-mile)

> **LOCALS' LORE:** *After numerous hard-fought reconnaissance expeditions, the first ascent of Assiniboine was finally accomplished, by Swiss guides Christian Bohren and Christian Häsler and their client James Outram, an English vicar who fell so in love with western Canada he eventually made his home here. The first winter ascent was accomplished in 1967 by Rockies locals Don Gardner, Eckhard Grassman and famed author and guide Chic Scott.*

route from Sunshine ski resort, plodding on as dusk fell. Suddenly, he unexpectedly intersected a freshly broken track at Og Meadows. When Gmoser and his group finally reached Assiniboine Lodge, Rummel was sitting by a window, waiting for them. She had broken the trail to make their long journey a bit easier.

Growing up 100 kilometres northeast of Switzerland's Matterhorn – to which Mount Assiniboine is frequently compared – Sepp Renner devoured Jack London's books and dreamed of going to Canada, "the land of adventure." With help from an uncle who was a professional mountain guide, Sepp earned his Swiss mountain guide's licence. He taught skiing at Quebec's Mont Tremblant in 1967 and in 1968 he reached Assiniboine's 3618-metre (11,870-foot) summit for the first of forty-eight times (as of winter 2011), with a client. With no work the following week, he offered to split wood for Strom.

"He must have thought I was alright, I knew how to split wood – being a farm boy," Sepp said with a laugh, taking a moment's break from the myriad chores associated with running the lodge.

For fourteen winters, Sepp guided heli-skiers at Hans Gmoser's Canadian Mountain Holidays lodges. Then in 1983, seeking a more family-friendly environment, he took over management of Assiniboine Lodge from Strom's daughter, Siri. Running the lodge with Sepp was his wife, Barb, and their three small children, André, Sara and Natalie. Before they could keep pace with the guests, André and his sisters raced each other on skis down the slope in front of the lodge. As Sara grew she earned her place on Canada's national cross-country ski team – and a silver medal with her teammate Beckie Scott in the sprint relay event at the 2006 Torino Winter Olympics.

"It was really nice having the kids grow up here," Sepp said. "At the beginning we were not that busy, so we spent a lot of time with the kids. At first it was just little hikes – Natalie was six, Sara was eight, André ten. I had to bring the teddy bears with me, and they had to look out of the pack."

The first summer, weekly supplies arrived by horseback, but when the pack train didn't show up one Tuesday, Sepp hiked over Allenby Pass to discover the cowboys had been partying the night before. Not amused, Sepp decided to hire more reliable, quicker and less expensive helicopters.

"Still, it was a sad moment to see the last pack train go around the corner," Sepp admitted.

By the time André was thirteen he'd begun working in the kitchen and helping guide guests. In 2004 he took over as full-time manager, while his dad continues to work there "off and on." André divides his time between Canmore and Radium, when he's not running the lodge from February to April for skiers and snowshoers, and mid-June to mid-October for hikers and climbers. He enjoys the rhythm of lodge work, maintaining the buildings, outhouses, sauna and woodshed – and caring for the guests.

"We see a lot of different people from all over the world," André said. "There are so many beautiful places you can go exploring. I'm still finding new variations, seeing different things each time. Overall, I think running the lodge has taught me to be a calm person. There is a lot to deal with, and only so much you can do. You just deal with it as it comes."

Living near Golden, BC, Natalie Renner is a paramedic and

A mid-winter sunrise lighting the summit of Mount Assiniboine is a welcome sight to skiers preparing for the day inside the historic lodge that bears the mountain's name.

an assistant ski guide who guides at the lodge part-time in winter.

Sara Renner remembers skiing the 28 kilometres out to Mount Shark when she was only seven, and she retains vivid memories of the family's first Christmas at the then uninsulated lodge, when –50°c (–58°f) temperatures necessitated sleeping on the dining room tables – the only room they could keep warm. Overnight, body heat glued the mattresses to the tables.

"The lodge has always been an incredible part of my life; it's helped make me who I am," Sara said. "To me, it feels like a family member; I really miss it when I'm gone, and when I'm there I feel whole again."

Sara and her husband, former Canadian alpine ski team member Thomas Grandi, have a daughter, Aria, who made her own first tracks on the slope in front of the lodge when she was only two, schussing in the family tradition.

History passed down through generations is part of what

makes Assiniboine Lodge such an invaluable treasure, insists Barb Renner. The highest peak in its namesake provincial park, Mount Assiniboine straddles the boundary of Banff National Park. Soaring 500 metres (1,640 feet) above any neighbouring peaks, the uniquely recognizable summit is also part of the Canadian Rocky Mountain UNESCO World Heritage Site. While the lodge is actually owned by the BC government, for the Renners it's been a very special home for the entire family.

"We've never owned it, but I think we've cared for it like we owned it," Barb said. "We've always strived to maintain some mechanism whereby its history will always be there. There are very few places left where you feel that kind of historic ambiance. It's always an interesting place, and it's the people who make it interesting. Up there, your relationships with people are quite different. The art of storytelling still exists in places like that. With no Internet or other distractions, our guests comment on how refreshing it is to come to a place that has changed so very little."

Best seasons: Mount Assiniboine Lodge is a true backcountry paradise that's open to hikers and mountaineers from mid-June to early October and for backcountry skiers from mid-February to early April. The lodge can be accessed by a short helicopter ride, or on foot or skis via several routes, the shortest of which is 28 kilometres (17 miles). Visit www.assiniboinelodge. com.

Trailhead: Mount Assiniboine Provincial Park can be accessed on foot or skis from the Sunshine Village ski area (29 kilometres/18 miles), via the Simpson River trailhead on Highway 93 South in Kootenay National Park (32 kilometres/20 miles), or from the Banff townsite via Brewster Creek/Allenby Pass (47 kilometres/29 miles). The most popular route is via Bryant Creek, starting at the Mount Shark trailhead. From Canmore, follow Spray Lakes Road, which becomes the Smith Dorrien–Spray Lakes Trail (Highway 742 South) for 37 kilometres (23 miles) to the Mount Shark Road turnoff.

Turn right and follow the road until it ends in a parking lot. From Calgary, follow the Trans-Canada Highway west to Highway 40. Turn south (left) and drive past Nakiska and Fortress ski hills to the Smith Dorrien–Spray Lakes/Highway 742 junction. Turn right (west) and soon after turn right again onto Highway 742. Drive about 30 kilometres (18.6 miles) north to Mount Shark Road. Turn left. Topo maps *Mount Assiniboine 82 J/13*, *Spray Lakes Reservoir 82 J/14*, *Banff 82 O/4* and, for approaching from the south by a difficult, off-trail route, *Tangle Peak 82 J/12*.

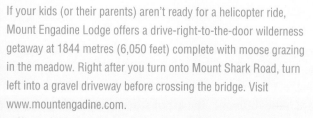

If your kids (or their parents) aren't ready for a helicopter ride, Mount Engadine Lodge offers a drive-right-to-the-door wilderness getaway at 1844 metres (6,050 feet) complete with moose grazing in the meadow. Right after you turn onto Mount Shark Road, turn left into a gravel driveway before crossing the bridge. Visit www.mountengadine.com.

If your kids are happy campers – or their parents are – Kananaskis Country is home to dozens of beautiful campsites equipped with a wide range of services. My favourite is Interlakes Campground, located on a thin strip of land separating Upper and Lower Kananaskis Lakes in Peter Lougheed Provincial Park, with easy access to hiking trails or the option of sitting by the shore of a sparkling turquoise glacier-fed lake with a good book. Check out www.kananaskiscountrycampgrounds.com.

Book your helicopter flight and spend a few days hiking across high alpine meadows, along jewel-toned tarns and amidst a kaleidoscope of lively wildflowers in the company of knowledgeable interpretive guides as guests of the utterly charming and comfortable Assiniboine Lodge, set in a lovely meadow at 2180 metres (7,200 feet). Bring an appetite! See www.assiniboinelodge.com.

If you're working with a leaner travel budget, or you prefer sleeping on the ground or in a very basic log cabin, you can fly into the area and camp at Lake Magog Campground or stay at the self-catered Naiset Cabins, a 15-minute walk from the lodge.

From the Mount Shark trailhead, hike to Mount Assiniboine via Bryant Creek, 28 kilometres (17 miles) with elevation gain of 455 metres (1,493 feet); or from Sunshine Village, 29 kilometres (18 miles), gaining 165 metres (541 feet).

If you want to give your back a break, you can send your gear in by helicopter while you hike or ski. Stay at Assiniboine Lodge, Naiset Cabins or camp, winter or summer, and explore the hiking trails or make some ski turns in untracked Rockies powder. All reservations can be made through www.assiniboinelodge.com.

Climb Mount Assiniboine, 3562 metres (11,686 feet) by its North Ridge (II, 5.5) or its Southwest Face (II), with an overnight at the R.C. Hind climbers' hut high above Lake Magog. For a complete route description, check out *The 11,000ers of the Canadian Rockies*, by Bill Corbett.

Hire a guide: If you don't have the requisite skills and experience, hire a guide to take you on any of these adventures or to organize a custom trip: www.assiniboinelodge.com.

3

K-Country Ridge Guards
Treasure Trove of Data

Walking uphill along the edge of a groomed ski run at Nakiska ski resort, I followed Dr. John Pomeroy, head of the University of Saskatchewan's Centre for Hydrology. With us were his research assistant Logan Fang, and field technician May Guan.

Each of us carried a backpack with lunch, hot Thermos, emergency layers and snowshoes, while the three researchers hiked with the added weight of equipment including scoops and cutters for measuring snow density, tool kit, a snow tube scale, keyboards and storage modules for downloading data, serial USB interfaces for dataloggers and even a laptop computer.

Since 2003, the IP3 (Improved Processes and Parameterization for Prediction in Cold Regions) research network has been conducting snowpack depth and density studies in Canada's cold regions, with sites at Marmot Creek in Kananaskis Country; Peyto Glacier and Lake O'Hara in the Rockies; Wolf Creek in the Yukon; Havikpak and Baker creeks in Northwest Territories; and Polar Bear Pass in Nunavut.

"The easy science has always been done in places that are easy to drive a truck up to," Pomeroy said. "Those places have years of detailed measurements. It's the Arctic and the higher elevations, the more remote areas, that have the big questions now.

We don't have nearly enough snow, glacier, water and weather observing stations in the Rockies. The region is undergoing rapid climate warming and changes to snowfall patterns, which are causing glacier retreat and shorter snow seasons and impairing the ability of river headwaters to generate reliable streamflow for vast downstream regions."

Those regions include the South Saskatchewan River Basin, which supplies water to much of the Prairies, and also the Athabasca River, which is a sub-basin of the Mackenzie River system – Canada's largest and second only to the Missouri/Mississippi in all of North America.

After an hour and a quarter of steady uphill walking on a track firmly packed with washboard snowmobile tracks, we stopped to strap on snowshoes, then continued along a narrow trail made by previous ski and snowshoe traffic. Passing a small clearing with a stick standing in the snow, Pomeroy explained how the Twin Creeks groundwater observation site was part of the Marmot Creek studies that were conducted between the 1960s and 1980s by the Canadian Forestry Service and Natural Resources Canada.

Minutes later, our packed trail ran out, and with the stamina of the Bow Valley's top athletes, Fang forged ahead, not slowed one bit by the hollow, 1.2-metre-long, 10-centimetre-diameter snow-density measuring tube he carried in his hand as he broke trail in the knee-deep, sugary eastern slopes Rockies snowpack. Winding around bushes, stepping over logs and ducking under deadfall blocking the trail like shoulder-high hurdles, we occasionally stopped to relocate the barely visible dent in the snowpack that marked the way.

"The first trip up after Christmas is always the toughest," Pomeroy said. "A few more trips and we'll have a highway."

Sure, albeit a highway navigable only by snowshoes that goes uphill for a gain of 800 metres (2,625 feet). As an avid mountaineer with considerable off-trail experience, I decided this was no beginner's snowshoeing trail, but a first-rate test of mountain fitness that would not be fun for anyone unaccustomed to hauling a backpack up mountainsides. I found myself chuckling at the thought of climate change deniers so gleefully firing off letters to the editor accusing "Climategate" scientists of fudging research data for the reward of increased funding.

No amount of funding, I concluded, would motivate any person to endure such a slog. While mountaineers push themselves up treadmill scree in pursuit of a summit, and backcountry skiers climb for hours for the fleeting reward of untracked powder turns, Pomeroy and his team will enthusiastically make this ascent repeatedly throughout the remainder of the winter for the simple reward of recording another week's worth of wind and precipitation data.

Fisera Ridge is named for Denny Fisera, who, through the 1970s, hiked up there every few days to check on dozens of hydrometric research sites run by the Canadian Forestry Service.

Finally reaching treeline three and a half hours after leaving the parking lot, Pomeroy checked the readings on a Weighing Geonor snow/rain gauge that resembled a 2-metre-tall (6½-foot) amusement park giant swing ride. The temperature read –3.5°C (25.7°F), the wind was blowing 3 metres (10 feet) per second from the south, humidity was 60 per cent. An aluminum ladder was propped against a tree, its base firmly buried in the snow. Most years, Pomeroy said, the snowpack would become so deep that they'd need the ladder to access the gauge. Not this year, though.

LOCALS' LORE: *The Centennial Ridge trail was built as the highest trail ever constructed in the Canadian Rockies by the Rocky Mountain Ramblers hiking group in celebration of Canada's 100th birthday in 1967. The work took three summers and culminated in a champagne ceremony on the summit during a typical Rockies midsummer snow squall.*

Continuing along the windswept ridge, Fang and Guan walked a transect line, measuring the snow depth every 5 metres (16 feet), and recording its weight every 20 metres (66 feet) using the snow tube Fang carried and a spring scale specially calibrated for the purpose. The deepest snow was 159 centimetres (63 inches), the shallowest 2 centimetres (0.8 inch).

We moved on to a smaller station on the north side of the ridge, then to one on the south, where the researchers plugged in USB cables and downloaded data. The information recorded gives them the ability to calculate the snow water equivalent (SWE, pronounced "swee"), the depth of water that would be standing if the snowpack were transformed to water – or the equivalent depth in rainfall.

"The trick was to keep a solar panel here that wouldn't blow away," Pomeroy said. "We had some disasters at first. The first one was attached to two sections of T bar – that's what cattle ranchers use. It got bent over by the wind. I'd never seen that before!"

The winds on Fisera Ridge regularly reach 150 kilometres (93 miles) per hour. The stunted, beaten krummholz are evidence of that.

Hanging at the far end of a steel pipe arm, two domes called radiometers measure solar radiation and thermo-infrared radiation, both coming in and going out. An ultrasonic snow-depth gauge bounces a signal off the snow to record its depth.

"It works like a rangefinder in an old Polaroid camera," Pomeroy explained. It also measures soil temperature, soil moisture and snow temperature. Each instrument on the metal frame is wired into a datalogger, a computer with a series of ports that applies voltage to the instruments for a few milliseconds and measures what comes back, in a manner similar to a voltmeter.

Measurements are taken every ten seconds, saved up in the datalogger's memory, averaged, and then stored in the datalogger permanent memory every fifteen minutes. Once a day the

Field technician May Guan, left, and research assistant Logan Fang use a snow-density measurement tube and a specially calibrated scale to record the weight of the snow at Fisera Ridge high above Nakiska ski hill.

datalogger uploads data to a website via a telemetry system. The data goes through a modem to a radio, which sends the numbers to a radio attached to another datalogger in a clearing at the Marmot Creek upper clearing site farther down the mountain. From there the data goes via cell phone to a web address.

The raw data can be read from a computer in Saskatoon, where Pomeroy was based at the University of Saskatchewan until relocating to Canmore in 2009 to be closer to his research sites. Remote sites such as this require regular and frequent monitoring. When an anemometer stopped transmitting wind-speed data from its perch on the roof of the Alpine Club of Canada's Bow Hut, for example, someone had to make the 8-kilometre (5-mile) ski up there to find out a wire was broken.

The computer in Saskatoon puts the data on a website, which Pomeroy had checked before we hiked up that morning.

Encased in a separate black box, a time-lapse camera is triggered by the datalogger to take two photos per day – late morning and early afternoon – of the snow-covered cirque below Mount Allan's summit.

"We're interested in the snow-covered area," Pomeroy said. "During the snowmelt, that tells us how much of the basin is melting and contributing to the stream flow. It's most important in May, June, July. This is the least amount of snow I've ever seen in all the years I've been coming here. We could be looking at the D-word – drought."

We'd only been at the site about ninety minutes when the sun dropped below the ridgeline a few hundred feet above us.

"Time to get the heck out of Dodge," Pomeroy said, packing up. "Once the sun goes down, it gets ugly up here."

I didn't doubt it, and he's got the data to prove it.

Even going downhill, it takes a full two hours to hike quickly back to the parking lot. No summit tagged, no fresh powder turns, no retention incentives, no performance bonuses. Just another tiny drop in the stream of hydrological research.

If, in your backcountry travels, you should ever come across a weather station or other scientific equipment, please respect those installations as the hard-won work of dedicated researchers who are studying these sites for the benefit of all of us. And while you can look and take pictures, *please don't touch anything!*

Trailhead: To reach Nakiska ski resort, Follow the Trans-Canada (east from Canmore or west from Calgary), to the Highway 40 junction. Drive south for 25 kilometres (15.5 miles) to Nakiska. Turn west onto Mount Allan Drive. Topo map *Spray Lakes Reservoir 82 J/14.*

Troll Falls Loop, 3.7 kilometres (2.3 miles), 30 metres (98 feet) elevation gain.

Once on Mount Allan Drive, go straight through the first junction, then turn right into the Stoney Trail parking lot. With a waterfall, winding creek, meadows and mini-caves comprising the troll's eye sockets, this short loop offers plenty of entertainment potential for hikers of all heights and ages.

Ribbon Falls, 9.4 kilometres (5.8 miles), 311 metres (1,020 feet) elevation gain, high point 2073 metres (6,801 feet).

Once on Mount Allan Drive, turn left onto Centennial Drive, then right onto Ribbon Creek Road. Drive past Kananaskis Wilderness Hostel to the Upper Ribbon Creek parking lot.

On foot or by mountain bike: For the first 4.3 kilometres (2.7 miles), Ribbon Falls offers a great day-hiking destination rewarded by the sight of a spectacular gushing waterfalls. For those with a little extra energy and enthusiasm, an exciting scramble up to Ribbon Lake via the steep cliffbands from which the falls tumble is facilitated by some very helpful chains permanently bolted into the rock.

Mount Allen Centennial Ridge traverse, 19 kilometres (12 miles), 1400 metres (4,593 feet) elevation gain, high point 2819 metres (9,249 feet).

You'll need two cars to make this trip work, one parked at the Pigeon Mountain parking lot, accessed by exiting the Trans-Canada Highway at Dead Man's Flats (25 kilometres, 15.5 miles, east of Canmore) and following a gravel road south for a short distance. Park the other car at Ribbon Creek parking lot (see Ribbon Falls hike, above) and start your hike here. Follow the signs to the Centennial Ridge summit, then continue northward along the ridgeline right through a fascinating collection of rock pinnacles. The trail down the north side of Mount Allan is a bit rough in places, but the route-finding is just interesting enough to be fun. The full traverse makes for an excellent day spent exploring quite a bit of high mountain terrain.

Mount Lorette, South Ridge, II, 5.4, high point 2469 metres (8,100 feet).

If you've got the rock-climbing skills, this is one fun, narrow, exposed ridge climb with just a few 5.4 rock moves. For a route description, check out *Selected Alpine Climbs in the Canadian Rockies*, by Sean Dougherty.

Deborah Skelton places a piece of climbing protection while leading an ascent of Mount Lorette in Kananaskis Country.

Hire a guide: If you don't have the requisite skills and experience to embark on this Front Range classic, hire a guide to take you on any of these adventures or to organize a custom trip: www.acmg.ca, www.yamnuska.com or www.internationalguidebureau.com.

Whitewater rafting and kayaking: Since its flow is dam controlled, the Kananaskis River remains at a constant Grade 2 to 3 whitewater level (for the flow schedule, see www.transalta.com). With such reliable, manageable waves, Canadian Rockies Rafting offers guided whitewater rafting trips for families with kids aged five and up: www.rafting.ca.

Experienced paddlers can put in at the Widowmaker (follow Highway 40 for 7.5 kilometres, 4.7 miles, south of the Trans-Canada Highway interchange) and surf standing waves such as the Green Tongue and Santa Claus as well as test their rodeo skills on a race course complete with slalom gates: http://paddlealberta.org.

Caving Reveals
Otherworldly Adventure

am crawling on hands and knees on a lumpy, brown-dirt
floor. At least my headlamp beam makes it appear brown.
The uneven surface is littered with rocks and boulders, everything smothered in a fine dust that permeates the cool air – the
floor, the boulders that restrict and channel my course of travel,
the walls, the low, vaulted stone ceiling.

I am grateful for my knee pads. And for my helmet. I'm so
absorbed by the floor that I don't look ahead often enough
to avoid collision with the irregular ceiling. Not that I would
see much anyway; my surroundings are limited to whatever is
illuminated by the narrow beam of light. Rounding a bend, I
lose sight of my companions. For a very long minute I can't
even hear them.

Just as space is obscured to me, so is time. I have no sense of
the hour, the day of the week, what season it might be outside
above my underground environs. Even through rubber-palmed
gloves, the ground feels cold and clammy as I weave around
small puddles like an oversized toddler. Eventually I rejoin
the group, their light beams illuminating the shadowy, other-
worldly cavern.

Spurred by the simple impulse of human curiosity, in 1883
three railway labourers stumbled upon a cave that contained a

pool of naturally warm sulphur water carved inside the lower slopes of Sulphur Mountain, at the edge of Banff townsite. Thinking they'd hit the motherlode that would bring them fame and especially fortune as the proprietors of a deluxe bathing resort, Frank McCabe and brothers William and Tom McCardell filed a claim in an attempt to acquire the land the springs bubbled within. Their plans were thwarted, however, as Canada's government and the Canadian Pacific Railway had already begun to conceive designating the spectacular land-scape of the area as a protected place that would draw lucrative tourist traffic, western settlement and valuable prestige on the international stage for the still-young country. Arguments over the ownership of the Banff Hot Springs escalated into a legal battle, which the Government of Canada eventually settled in 1885 by declaring that the coveted springs would belong to all Canadians as the country's first – and North America's second, after Yellowstone – national park.

Today's modern cavers, or spelunkers, are as curious as ever. Spurred by their sense of adventure with few entrepreneurial designs, they employ safe rope and travel techniques to explore the underground as enthusiastically as weekend rock climbers. While very real dangers do exist, serious accidents are fortu-nately rare.

LOCALS' LORE: *Dedicated cavers routinely embark on 14-hour outings; and as with mountaineering, reaching the summit – or the bottom – is only half the trip.* "Caving is more demanding than most outdoor activi-ties, with the exception of mountaineering," *says Canmore's Jon Rollins, a veteran spelunker and author of* Caves of the Canadian Rockies and Columbia Mountains. "It requires a lot of energy outlay for long periods of time and there's a good chance of being cold, wet and uncomfortable." *As for being comfortable in confined places, most cavers don't have any problems with it and are subjected to really small places for brief periods of time.* "If it doesn't bother you, it doesn't bother you," *Rollins says.*

I'd already experienced an adventure-filled summer, including an especially memorable climb of Mount Tupper in BC's Glacier National Park, which had forced me to overcome my fear on the scariest exposed cliff sections I've ever peered down from. Still, I felt ready for a new challenge. Following our Canmore Caverns guide, Eli, I joined a Rat's Nest Cave tour with six others. Hiking along the half-hour approach trail near my hometown of Canmore, I listened as two new acquaintances, Ryan and Angelina, a lively pair of late-twentysomethings, described their recent skydiving experience. Although I'm adventurous by some standards, I realized I'm not the thrill-seeking type. My adventures are motivated by a desire to explore fascinating wilderness landscapes. Caving, I would discover, reveals entirely different dimensions of landscapes.

As we donned our tour-supplied coveralls, climbing harnesses, knee pads and miner's-lamp-equipped helmets, Eli described how the Pleistocene glaciations of the past 1.6 million years caused meltwater to carve out the 4-kilometre-long (2.5-mile) Rat's Nest Cave system in the soft limestone. With a constant air temperature of 4.5°C (40°F), and descending 245 metres (804 feet) below its entrance, Canada's 11th longest – of 100 caves stretching more than 440 metres (1,444 feet) – is also the Canadian Rockies' warmest.

Halfway along our hike, Eli had stopped.

"We're standing 30 metres (98 feet) above the cave's largest room, the Grand Gallery," he said.

"How do you map a cave?" I asked.

"Compass and a measuring tape," he replied.

Stepping through the creaky access gate, Eli gave us the "cave rules": keep your head low, don't try to move too quickly and don't leave anything behind. In the entrance he pointed out ancient red pictographs on the wall, then gestured toward a dark, bottomless hole. The Bone Bed Pit contains artifacts including 3,000-year-old arrowheads, likely left behind by Aboriginal peoples seeking shelter in the entranceway.

To preserve this important paleontological site from rope-equipped souvenir seekers, in 1987 one square mile around the entrance was designated a Provincial Historic Site, complete with locked access gate.

Stooping and lurching deeper into the cave, Eli demonstrated how to clip ourselves into the safety rope as we slid down a smooth, polished rock ramp into the next chamber. Regrouping in a classroom-sized space, he pointed to another hole in the floor, telling us we'd exit the cave through there later.

It looked pretty darned small.

As we moved to the next section, the roof began slanting lower and lower until we stopped, wedged on our sides into a passage barely a metre (three feet) at its highest. After clipping himself into a climbing anchor permanently bolted into the rock, Eli supervised as, one by one, we clipped into the double safety rope system to rappel down into a 20-metre (66-foot) vertical abyss. Relieved to be released from my cramped position, at my turn I eagerly lowered myself into the industrial-elevator-sized pit walled with moist, slick rock.

With everyone down the well-hole, we reached our first optional "small squeeze" – caving lingo for a small, constricted space.

"It's more fun if you go headfirst," Eli suggested.

"Headfirst, you say? Okay!" chirped Angelina, already slithering on her belly through a passage at floor level, just high enough to swallow her head, torso, legs and finally her feet.

Not quite headfirst I wriggled my way through the crawl space sideways, employing a crab-like manoeuvre that got me onto a shelf that dropped under my left leg like a staircase step. I felt grateful for years of yoga classes.

Entering the Five-Way Chamber, Eli suggested we all remember this room, since it was the only access to the cave exit. As he said this, I realized we were immersed in a labyrinth with countless dead ends and few clues for the untrained eye to landmark. My perception was distorted; distance was difficult to judge. I was certain my boots would slip in places they didn't, and the floor appeared steeper than it actually was. With no plants, no wind, no sky and no horizon, the world was reduced to what appeared directly in front of our light bulbs.

Then we reached the Laundry Chute.

"This is our next optional squeeze," Eli announced.

Anyone who didn't feel comfortable could wait at that spot for fifteen minutes until the group looped back up, Eli suggested. He described a body-sized vertical tube that dropped for 3 metres (10 feet), then dog-legged into a 45°, equally snug 6-metre (20-foot) tunnel before opening into the next stand-able room.

"Thirty feet in thirty seconds," Eli grinned with a wink. "I'm sure you'll all fit."

While the others jostled to go first, I wondered why I couldn't be the kind of person content to seek out simple "fun fun" rather than "good-grief-this-is-an-uncomfortable-challenge fun." Determined not to be left alone, I settled midway into the queue with giant butterflies lurching in my gut.

Sliding up to the hole, Erem dropped one leg down, followed by the other. With his arms reaching one above and one below him, he inched his body down into a space so constricted I could not see beyond him as he was swallowed by the earth.

My turn.

While I rationally understood I could be free of the squeeze in less than a minute, and that hundreds of cavers much larger than my size-6 body had previously fit through, I battled my imagination. Unlike negotiating some alpine terrain where a mistake would guarantee a death fall, I recognized the hazards of this challenge existed largely in my mind. I knew I must banish all thoughts of things beyond my control, mainly the infinitesimally tiny possibility of an earth tremor, the only thing that could realistically, on this guided tour, trap me to suffer an unthinkable fate.

A caver lowers into a "squeeze" called the Laundry Chute deep inside Rat's Nest Cave.

Grateful for my athletic strengths, I soon realized I was even more thankful for how twenty years of outdoor challenges had prepared me for the mental control this situation demanded of me. I lowered myself into the shaft, at times so tight I was forced to turn my head sideways to make space for the headlamp protruding from it. I moved a lot by feel, since I was rarely able to see my next footstep. For a brief moment the passage opened large enough for me to sit. Then I shimmied into the chute section, quickly experiencing the wedgie Eli had promised.

Following voices ahead of me, I slithered down to a fork in the human-diameter pipe, fortunately remembering Eli's instructions to stay left and not be suckered into the large-ended funnel tube on my right where my worst fears of becoming trapped would be realized. Bumping and sliding, one foot, then my butt, one shoulder, then the other arm, I couldn't move fast enough in a place where fast wasn't an option as I focused on staying ahead of thoughts I did not want to entertain.

Finally free, my chicken-in-a-foreign-environment voice in my head was adamant that I never had to make myself do that again. My cocky-adventurous voice in my head however, expressed excited congratulations.

Walking erect through the next passage, Eli described a section deeper into the cave that remained as tight as the Laundry Chute for an hour. And a half. Still babbling with anxiety, I had to ask: "Head or feet first?"

Soon, our journey revealed the fascinating landscape rewards that so motivate and enrapture me. Calcite deposits exquisitely sculpted by nature appeared – the Wedding Cake, a multi-tiered, melted-wax-like stalagmite; and the Bacon Strip, hanging like a calcite slab of cured meat. In another chamber, hundreds of hollow "soda straw" stalactites clung delicately from the ceiling, each one remarkably resembling its moniker.

"They grow one centimetre [half an inch] a year – as fast as anything around here," Eli said.

Next we reached the Grand Gallery, where two distinct sheets of rock intersected at the perfectly peaked ceiling, at places 30 metres (98 feet) high.

"It's a perfect fault line, where the mountains shifted and ground together," Eli explained.

I sincerely hoped they would wait another day to do that again.

A caver drops deeper into The Grotto, one chamber inside Rat's Nest Cave.

The Grand Gallery led to The Grotto, where the mini-cathedral's walls were adorned with flowstone formations preserved like dribbled candle wax, with two small, crystal-clear ponds scooped into the floor. The utterly exotic room reminded me of a friendly version of the hatching chamber from the movie *Alien*.

"Now, everyone, turn off your headlamps," Eli directed.

Breathing as quietly as possible, we tuned in to the musical plinking of water trickling in the absolute darkness. Realizing my eyes were closed, I opened them, but there was no difference. I had no concept of anything except my body standing in profound darkness.

I never did recognize the Five-Way Chamber when we re-entered it about an hour later, but fortunately Eli did, leading us up a corridor of easy boulders until we arrived at a wonky chute of rough and ill-matched two-by-four ladder steps. Climbing the staircase that had been excavated by crowbar-wielding cavers a few years back, I emerged through a tiny hole in the floor of the higher, classroom-sized chamber I did recognize, feeling like a POW from *The Great Escape*.

Stepping through the creaky iron entrance gate, I snuck a glance back at the cave. My cocky-adventurous voice in my head shouted a big thumbs-up.

Best seasons: Since the temperature inside Rat's Nest Cave is constant, Canmore Caverns runs tours all year round, which makes it an ideal activity even when it's –30°C (–22°F) in the dead of winter. For a range of tours for various levels of fitness and curiosity, visit www.canmorecavetours.com.

Trailhead: Canmore Caverns' guided tours begin and end in the Sobeys parking lot on Railway Avenue in Canmore. Topo map *Canmore 82 O/3*.

Children 10 and older are welcome to join Caverns tours, but if you're looking for an interesting adventure for younger kids – or claustrophobic bigger kids – bring a flashlight or headlamp and explore a man-made tunnel drilled into the north-facing lower slope of Mount McGillivray. Accessed by parking on the north side of the Trans-Canada opposite Lac des Arcs and walking up a short hiking trail, the tunnel is the remnant of a fallout shelter partially constructed by a private company hoping to sell storage space in the event of a nuclear attack circa the late 1950s, a project that made perfect sense during the height of the Cold War. To learn more, visit www.highlineonline.ca/media/winter_2009/exposure/dark_secret. html.

Canmore Caverns' Explorer Tour will take you inside Rat's Nest Cave for two and a half hours, where you'll climb, crawl, slither and wriggle your way down to the sparkling pool surrounded by walls dripping with stalactites in the Grotto. And back up, of course.

Sign on for the full-meal-deal Adventure Tour, and experience all of the above plus an 18-metre (59-foot) rappel and the Laundry Chute!

Offered only during the summer, if you're a fit, strong and experienced backcountry camper and you know for certain you're comfortable exploring dark, confined spaces for extended periods, sign up for Canmore Caverns' three-day Alpine Caving Adventure to the Cleft and Gargantua caves in the Crowsnest Pass region of the southern Alberta Rockies: www.canmorecavetours.com.

Mountain biking: Don't miss the Canmore Nordic Centre's 60 kilometres (37 miles) of rolling doubletrack and test-piece single-track trails: www.canmoreadventures.ca. The host facility for cross-country skiing and biathlon events for the 1988 Winter Olympics is also home to 65 kilometres (40 miles) of impeccably groomed cross-country skiing trails: www.tpr.alberta.ca.

Canyon Guide Reveals Classroom Treasures

"The nice thing about wandering about these mountains is that they are the greatest classroom in the world," declared Ward Cameron as he led a group of hikers along the snow- and ice-plastered path of Johnston Canyon, a twenty-minute drive west of Banff, one January morning.

A naturalist, historian and tour guide with more than twenty-five years' experience in the Canadian Rockies, Cameron enthusiastically shared his favourite classroom as the path merged onto a concrete walkway rimmed with iron railings and suspended above a fascinating wonderland of gurgling creeks, frosty snow bridges and ice curtains dripping from the vertical canyon walls.

Guiding for a Canadian Rockies Rafting privately booked canyon tour, Cameron started out by equipping his dozen clients with adjustable ice cleats, which fit over everyone's winter boots. Within minutes we'd forgotten what otherwise would be a treacherous surface underfoot, and listened intently as Cameron revealed one treasure after another that we likely wouldn't have noticed without him.

"This canyon is just a fabulous walk in an icy landscape that lets you see what you don't normally see," said Cameron, who still recalls his first canyon tour as a novice interpretive guide

Ward Cameron

in 1982. "In winter, the canyon is constantly changing. The ice is not a static feature – particularly with waterfalls."

Frozen waterfalls change with the temperature, sometimes forming thin curtains behind which water splashes and bubbles, much like a forceful tap behind a sheer shower curtain – a phenomenon that was plentiful the day we visited.

On a more evolutionary scale, however, Cameron explained the canyon's waterfalls are constantly changing as water erodes layers of soft rock sitting underneath layers of much more durable rock.

"In order to have a waterfall persist in nature over time, you need to have a layer of hard rock sitting over a layer of softer rocks," he explained. "Water will flow over the lip of the harder rock, and cause the softer layer below to wear away. Eventually, you get an overhang. That's why you often find caves behind waterfalls. Dippers build their nests there, where they are safe from predators."

Over time the lip will collapse and the waterfall moves upstream, starting the process all over again.

"Which explains why so often you have a canyon in front of a waterfall," he continued. "As we climb up the canyon it's like a staircase of waterfalls."

Johnston Canyon's first set of falls presents a perfect example with a perfectly formed plunge pool set in the riverbed about 15 metres (49 feet) ahead of the present-day waterfall.

But ice and waterfalls are only a small part of the picture unfolding in the canyon, Cameron pointed out, particularly once the snow falls.

"In summertime, we are often aware of the presence of herbivores, particularly deer and elk," he said. "But we don't see the carnivores. The nice thing about winter, nothing can go

LOCALS' LORE: *The steep, mossy walls behind the Upper Falls are home to nearly 30 endemic species of algae. Keep your eyes open for dippers swooping from one canyon wall to the other. Also, the canyon is one of only two known nesting sites in Alberta for the black swift. Also, on June 13, 2007, Canmore native Logan Grayling, already an experienced whitewater kayaker at the age of 19, launched his kayak off the lip of the Upper Falls and plunged 30.5 metres (100 feet) to a "really soft" landing in the frothing pool below. Read the full story in my book* Expedition to the Edge: Stories of Worldwide Adventure.

outside without leaving evidence of its passing. Very quickly, you become aware you are not alone."

With that, he pointed out a set of pine marten tracks, easily identified by their unique offset two-by-two pawprints.

"In this canyon, the pine marten is your constant companion, but I rarely see other weasels," Cameron said. "They take advantage of the forest's older growth, which gives them lots of deadwood to hide under, where they can snack on mice and voles that travel through the understorey by tunnelling under the snow."

Asked to choose a favourite time to visit the canyon, Cameron didn't hesitate. "I love when my group is first up after a snowfall," he said. "It's more work breaking trail, but you know all those tracks are really fresh. When you come back down the walk, sometimes you find pine marten tracks on top of your own tracks. You know he's probably watching you. For me, it's a real treat to share a trail with them. That's what's great about winter; it brings more intimacy, different perspectives. The mountains aren't always about everything we can see."

Best season: Johnston Canyon is accessible – and delightful – all year round, so any time is a good time to follow the suspended walkway and take the time to read the interpretive panels that will open your eyes to the multi-dimensional world of a poster-child limestone canyon. The creek's water level is likely to be at its highest in early summer, when the runoff from snowmelt reaches its peak, but by then the crowds will have arrived as well. If you don't like crowds, visit during the fall, between Thanksgiving (mid-October in Canada) and the Christmas holiday season. Be sure to bring ice cleats, though. A slip the wrong way could have very serious consequences, or worse. In winter, walking up to the Upper Falls will allow you to watch ice climbers practise their sport on frozen waterfalls. To sign up for an interpretive tour, contact www.wardcameron.com. To book a stay right at the canyon, visit www.johnstoncanyon.com. To stay at HI-Castle Mountain wilderness hostel, visit www.hihostels.ca.

Trailhead: Exit the Trans-Canada Highway 5.5 kilometres (3.4 miles) west of the Mount Norquay interchange (west exit from Banff townsite). Follow the Bow Valley Parkway, Highway 1A, for 18 kilometres (11 miles) to the Johnston Canyon parking lot. Topo maps *Banff 82 O/4, Castle Mountain 82 O/5.*

Lower Falls, 1.1 kilometres (0.7 miles), minimal elevation gain.

Keep hold of your little ones' hands as you follow this sturdy catwalk with iron railings to the thundering Lower Falls, complete with an up-close, guaranteed-to-splash-you viewing point accessed through a mini-tunnel.

Upper Falls, 2.7 kilometres (1.7 miles).

Continue past the Lower Falls all the way to the spectacular 30-metre (100-foot) Upper Falls.

Ink Pots, 6 kilometres (3.7 miles), 215 metres (705 feet) elevation gain, high point 1645 metres (5,397 feet).

Only the diameter of small ponds, these deep-turquoise springs maintain a constant temperature of 4°C (39°F) and have bottoms composed of quicksand. Explore the trails of this upper valley and pick a lovely quiet spot for a picnic lunch.

Alternatively, launch your overnight backpacking trip from here and hike over Mystic Pass to Mount Norquay, 31.5 kilometres (20 miles), or dig up the maps *Banff 82 O/4, Castle Mountain 82 O/5, Lake Louise 82 N/8* and hike the Sawback Trail for two to four days all the way to Skoki (*The Canadian Rockies Trail Guide*, by Brian Patton and Bart Robinson).

Ice climbing: Swing your ice-climbing tools on routes ranging from Grade 2 beginner-angled ice to demanding WI5 climbs on a 60-metre-wide (197-foot) wall of ice 10 to 40 metres (33 to 131 feet) high.

Hire a guide: If you don't have the requisite skills and experience, hire a guide to take you on any of these adventures or to organize a custom trip: www.acmg.ca, www.yamnuska.com, www.internationalguidebureau.com or http://rockies-ice.com.

Work Crew Builds Hut amid Newborn Forest

Long before the breakfast dishes were washed, the Fay Hut construction camp sprang to life with the sounds of work being done. The generator hummed, hammers knocked on wood and the whine of a chainsaw echoed off the cliffs towering above the site.

In the background, chirping birds and the rush of a creek tumbling over a series of waterfalls reminded the group of volunteer carpenters and labourers of their spectacular surroundings. Five hundred metres (1,640 feet) above the floor of Prospectors Valley in Kootenay National Park, the high forest floor was a profusion of bright new greenness and brilliant wildflowers sprouting amid ghostly, fire-charred tree poles.

In the kitchen – a floorless canvas tent equipped with a fridge and a full-sized propane stove erected next to a dining tent furnished with four picnic tables, basic wood shelves and a pot-bellied, wood-burning stove – Val Weed mixed up muffin batter for the mid-morning coffee break. Soon the aroma of fresh baking filled the tents. Outside, the smell of freshly cut wood blended with potent hints of gasoline, and a small brush fire tended to rid the area of debris left by the forest fire that had consumed the valley – and the original Fay Hut – in August 2003.

Scramblers follow the well-worn upper section of the route to Mount Temple's 3543-metre (11,624-foot) summit.

LOCALS' LORE: *Prospectors Valley was named by Walter Wilcox, a wealthy Yale University graduate who made numerous visits to the Canadian Rockies, after he discovered an old prospectors camp at the valley's mouth. Wilcox hired outfitters to assist him on many productive exploratory expeditions and mountaineering adventures in the Rockies, including the first ascent of Mount Temple, 3543 metres (11,624 feet), the most visible of the Rockies' 54 peaks above 11,000 feet, and the second highest of the peaks situated entirely within Banff National Park.*

Constructed in 1927, Fay Hut was named for Charles Fay, founder of the American Alpine Club and an ardent fan of and frequent visitor to the Canadian Rockies. It was the first hut built and operated by the Alpine Club of Canada.*

*Now run by the Alpine Club of Canada, the older Elizabeth Parker and Abbot Pass huts, located in neighbouring Yoho National Park, were built in 1919 and 1922, respectively, by Swiss mountain guides on behalf of their employer, the Canadian Pacific Railway.

Makalu Designs' Carol Beaton, a Canmore slate and tile designer, created a unique stamp on the new Fay Hut's floor. Sadly, the log cabin burned down in April 2009.

The single-room, timber-frame cabin was engulfed within minutes when the Tokumm Creek fire rampaged through the valley, leaving little more than a few shards of glass and sections of the woodstove's metal chimney.

A semi-retired social worker from Prince George, BC, Val Weed was one of more than 100 ACC members who volunteered a week or two of their 2005 summer vacation to build a new log cabin to replace Fay Hut, including its cupboards, tables and upstairs sleeping room, outhouse, walking trails and grey-water pit.

Val served as volunteer cook for that week's work crew, and her years of experience cooking for groups at backcountry lodges and on remote Yukon canoe trips were enormously appreciated.

While the crew included two professional log builders from Calgary, many of the carpenters and labourers were volunteers, some of whom had helped build other Alpine Club huts that are enjoyed by thousands of hikers, climbers and backcountry skiers annually.

With the ACC poised to celebrate its centennial in 2006, the rebuilding project had been enthusiastically embraced and had even attracted significant cash donations toward construction costs. Led by club member Bruce Hardardt working as project manager, key volunteers had met twice a month for six months prior to the construction start date, coordinating the work teams, construction assistants, camp managers, cooks, trail crews, architects' drawings, Parks Canada permits and fundraising efforts.

After weeks of sending out requests for proposals from log builders, Dan Strand Log Homes of Calgary was awarded the contract. Because no helicopter time was available in July, the team worked weekends and evenings to complete construction before the scheduled mid-June flight date. The pieces were loaded onto a flatbed truck and taken to the Paint Pots trailhead parking lot in Kootenay National Park.

The physical work on Fay Hut began with a two-day blitz, with ten volunteers and two helicopters working ten-hour days to sling eighty-five loads of building supplies to the site from the staging area, which at the start resembled a massive construction yard. A third day was spent building the foundation, while work to assemble the fifty-eight precut logs into a two-storey cabin began in early July and continued through the month.

Building a log cabin in such a remote location – a 13-kilometre (8-mile) hike from Highway 93 South – presented some unique challenges, said log builder James Heck as he rested after a well-earned camp dinner.

"This is the first time I've ever had to put up a house away from my crane," Heck said. "I've got a couple of old crappy cranes at home that I wouldn't usually bother looking at, but I'd love to have one of them up here. But instead we're using some creative manpower."

One of the other volunteers, Val's husband, Jim Weed, was a retired heavy-duty mechanic who had spent his summers twenty-five years earlier building log houses.

"I'm used to this," Weed grinned. "That's where I learned the bootstrap and leverage methods."

Their creation, the "Jim Weed crane," resembled a cross between a giant tripod and a deep-sea fishing rig, constructed of sturdy wooden beams, some metal braces and a hand-operated winch with steel cable.

With seven ground-floor windows, including one over-sized bay window overlooking the rock wall towering above Tokumm Creek, the new Fay Hut would sleep twelve, as the original did, but upstairs, with a much brighter downstairs cooking and common room.

Relaxing at the end of another long and gratefully dry work day – the first week's construction crew had tolerated daily showers and record-breaking downpours – the volunteers gathered in the dining tent to share dinner, rousing card games and stories about climbing adventures and backcountry trips to other remote mountain huts.

The volunteers came from cities across Canada, including Calgary, Whistler, Kimberley, BC, and Granby, Quebec. They included a lawyer, a financial planner, a retired high school science teacher and a mechanic aspiring to become a police officer.

Eighteen-year-old Montreal student and lifeguard Glen Robitaille had read about the project in the ACC's newsmagazine, the *Gazette*, and immediately decided how to spend his summer vacation.

"I stayed at the old Fay Hut," Robitaille said. "Building the new one seemed like it would be a fun project."

Wearing the same blue plaid lumberjack shirt he wore to build the University of BC's Whistler Cabin in 1965, retired geologist Karl Ricker recounted a climbing trip in the Fay Hut area in 1958 when he and a partner climbed up a gully from Moraine Lake, thinking it was the then popular 3/4 Couloir. Only at the top did they realize that in the poor visibility they'd made what was likely the second ascent of the next gully

Gail Crowe-Swords savours the view from Fay Hut during a backcountry skiing trip in February 2006, a few months after it was built in the summer of 2005.

to the south. After topping out on the glacier, they hiked down past the original Fay Hut, hoping to make it to the highway, but when their headlamps no longer illuminated the forest they ended up sleeping under a spruce tree.

Ricker helped build his first hut in 1953 and had worked on several since, including helping to renovate the ACC's Stanley Mitchell Hut in Little Yoho Valley in the 1980s.

"Once you start building huts it's hard to stop," Ricker said. "You're outside with all your friends and it's always a challenge. Nothing ever fits, or is square or something is missing. But it feels good to be doing something useful. And I wanted to see this valley again."

AUTHOR'S NOTE: *Sadly, sometime between 11 a.m. on April 2 and the evening of April 4, 2009, the second Fay Hut was incinerated.*

Investigators determined the cause of the fire was likely a design flaw that allowed drifted snow to push the chimney pipe against the wood of the roof beams, reducing the beams' ignition temperature over time until the wood caught fire. Plans for the ACC to build another log cabin at that location, which draws fewer visitors than other Canadian Rockies locations, are unlikely.

On a happier note, on February 16, 2010, Karl Ricker's daughter, Maëlle, won gold in the boarder cross event of the 2010 Vancouver Winter Olympics, becoming the first Canadian woman to win Olympic gold on home soil.

Best seasons: Although there is no longer a hut to provide warm and cozy overnight accommodations for backpackers and backcountry skiers, the valley can still be enjoyed by hikers and cross-country tourers keen to explore the valley bottom for a day trip. Summer hikers will particularly appreciate the fascinating post-fire forest environment.

Trailhead: From the Trans-Canada Highway, exit at the Castle Junction interchange and follow Highway 93 South to the Marble Canyon parking area 7 kilometres (4.3 miles) west of the Banff/Kootenay park boundary at the Continental Divide. Topo maps *Mount Goodsir 82 N/1, Lake Louise 82 N/8.*

Family Friendly

Marble Canyon interpretive trail, 800 metres (0.5 mile) one way, minor elevation gain.

This self-guided trail was rebuilt after the 2003 Tokumm Creek fire and weaves its way back and forth across the gushing creek that has carved the 40-metre-deep (131-foot) gorge into walls of limestone and dolomite, some of which is white and resembles marble.

Sweat a Little

Tokumm Creek, 10.5 kilometres (6.5 miles), high point about the same as the trailhead, 1490 metres (4,888 feet). Tokumm is the Stoney word for red fox.

Since the 2003 fire, the first few kilometres of this hike reveal the fascinating world of a forest in adolescent regrowth. Following the gravel flats alongside Tokumm Creek from the 10.4-kilometre mark, the trail climbs steeply for 2.5 kilometres (1.6 miles) to the old Fay Hut site or continues along the river for another 3 kilometres (2 miles) to where it begins the steep climb to Kaufmann Lake.

Kaufmann Lake, 15 kilometres (9.3 miles), elevation gain 570 metres (1,870 feet), high point 2060 metres (6,759 feet).

With the Wenkchemna Peaks as a backdrop, Kaufmann Lake is a lovely destination for an overnight backpacking trip to a secluded backcountry campground.

Neil Colgan Hut, 2940 metres (9,646 feet), the highest permanent structure in Canada: www.alpineclubofcanada.ca.

Tucked between mounts Little and Bowlen, also known as Peaks 2 and 3 when viewed from Moraine Lake, Neil Colgan Hut is accessible from the old Fay Hut site for mountaineers experienced in glacier travel and off-trail route-finding. In recent decades, the hut is more commonly reached via the Perren or Schiesser ledges mountaineering routes, both of which involve glacier travel and 1067 metres (3,500 feet) elevation gain. The basic 18-person hut provides ready access to numerous peaks, including Mount Fay, 3235 metres (10,614 feet). For route descriptions check out *Selected Alpine Climbs in the Canadian Rockies*, by Sean Dougherty.

Ice and mixed climbing: Marble Canyon and Haffner Creek, accessed by a 20-minute hike directly across Highway 93 (south side), offer dozens of pick-dulling bolted routes ranging from M5 to M10 for fit and flexible mixed ice climbers. See *Mixed Climbs in the Canadian Rockies*, by Sean Isaac.

Hire a guide: If you don't have the requisite skills and experience, hire a guide to take you on any of these adventures or to organize a custom trip: www.acmg.ca, www.yamnuska.com, www.internationalguidebureau.com or http://rockies-ice.com.

Stanley Mitchell Hut
a Welcome Refuge

During the summer of 1938, the executive committee members of the Alpine Club of Canada settled on a design for a new backcountry hut. But with plans drawn up, permission granted from the Dominion Parks Department (now known as Parks Canada), and sufficient funds available, the club encountered its greatest obstacle.

Good log men were becoming scarcer and scarcer, and the men the ACC wanted to hire weren't interested.

Apart from the fact that those builders were busy, a key reason for their refusal was the hut's location: 23 long kilometres (14 miles) from the Trans-Canada Highway up the Yoho River in Little Yoho Valley, just west of the Alberta/BC boundary in Yoho National Park.

Fortunately, the following summer Cyril Wates, who served as ACC president from 1938 through 1941, mentioned the dilemma while spending an evening with friends. His host quickly declared, "I'll get you a good man!"

Mr. H.A. Dowler of Mulhurst, Alberta, was not only an experienced log worker but also a former ACC member who had qualified for membership* by climbing a 3048-metre (10,000-foot) mountain at the club's Rogers Pass Camp in 1908. Dowler enthusiastically accepted the job.

* From its inception in 1906 until 1985, the Alpine Club of Canada required members to climb four mountains higher than 3048 metres (10,000 feet) in order to attain Active, or Senior, membership status.

Despite a late start due to heavy snowstorms and complications from the necessity of using unseasoned logs, the hut was completed in October 1939. Well conceived, well executed and wisely located at the edge of a meadow with a splendid view of the President and Vice President peaks, the hut was even finished under budget. It was promptly named for long-time ACC member Stanley Mitchell in recognition of his generous contributions as a volunteer and especially his popularity with novice climbers, including Montreal's Helen Trenholme, who donated $1,500 toward the hut's construction in gratitude for Mitchell's care and patience.

In summertime, Stanley Mitchell Hut is most commonly accessed by entire families via a well-graded 9.5-kilometre (5.9-mile) trail starting from the Takakkaw Falls parking area, or by the spectacularly scenic 10.7-kilometre (6.6-mile) Iceline Trail.

In winter, however, reaching the hut requires slightly more commitment. One option popular with experienced mountaineers and backcountry ski tourers is the 20-kilometre (12-mile) Bow–Yoho traverse. Starting from Bow Hut, the route crosses the Wapta Icefield and often involves a night of camping on the des Poilus Glacier, as well as navigating an icefall below Mount Collie where crevasses large enough to swallow a minivan lurk – a particularly exciting experience in frequent whiteouts.

The other most commonly followed approach is to ski the 23 kilometres (14 miles) from the Trans-Canada Highway to the hut, since the 13-kilometre (8-mile) section to Takakkaw Falls, which supports an endless train of motorhomes through the summer months, is not plowed in winter.

Having already skied the Bow–Yoho traverse in a whiteout in 2008 (which leaves it on my to-do-again-under-clear-skies bucket list), I decided it was time to tackle the 23-kilometre (14-mile) Takakkaw Falls–Yoho Valley option, so I posted the trip, with myself as volunteer leader/organizer, on the ACC's Rocky Mountain Section winter trip schedule.

LOCALS' LORE: *Yoho Valley was the site of the Alpine Club of Canada's inaugural climbing camp, which took place in July 1906, launching the club's continuing tradition of annual mountaineering camps. More than 100 members of the four-month-old organization paid $1 a day to sleep in some 40 canvas tents carried in by horseback along with cooking supplies, bedding, "proper attire" for Sunday mass, climbing ropes and appropriate clothing and hob-nailed boots, and to be led safely to the summits of the Vice President and other peaks by Swiss mountain guides. A plaque at Yoho Lake commemorates the ACC's Centennial in 2006.*

While some of my regular ski-touring partners grimaced at my chosen access route, four complete strangers e-mailed with expressions of interest. I inquired as to their previous trip experience, particularly in terms of long days, which I knew our approach route would demand. (On my aforementioned winter visit, it had taken our group seven hours to complete the mostly flat and otherwise downhill ski out from hut to highway.)

Knowing the recent warm, sunny days had the potential to turn the access road to mush, five of us left the parking lot just before 8 a.m. one day in early March, delighted that the valley bottom temperatures registered well below zero (32°F).

By noon we stopped for a leisurely lunch in the snow-blanketed Takakkaw Falls parking lot, opposite the very frozen and still waterfall, which, in its spectacular liquid form, elicits exclamation of wonder and awe from thousands of international tourists every summer.

With me were Chris, a sometime forest ranger from Vermont; Nic, a retired teacher and tireless adventurer from Canberra, Australia; and Beth and Earl from Jasper, Alberta. Impressively, Earl accomplished our entire four-day trip on a split board – a snowboard that can be separated into two halves to skin up, then reassembled into one board to make downhill turns.

Skier Beth Dauk follows the snow-covered Takakkaw Falls road on the 23-kilometre ski trip to Yoho's Stanley Mitchell Hut.

To our relief, the spring-like sun never softened the trail more than a little, and nearly nine hours after starting out, all five of us were happily shedding our packs, lighting a fire in the woodstove and precariously fishing for water from the nearby creek that trickled at the bottom of a steep and slippery snowbank to make tea and warm up our dehydrated dinners. The toil of our approach was quickly forgotten.

> A tour to the Little Yoho Valley is the quintessential Canadian Rockies skiing experience and is highly recommended. The hut is rarely crowded and anyone who can make it this far into the backcountry is usually a true mountain lover.

So wrote Canada's premier mountain writer Chic Scott in his guidebook *Summits & Icefields: Alpine Ski Tours in the Canadian Rockies.*

Among those true mountain lovers was Hans Gmoser, known for launching the helicopter skiing industry, and, with long-time friend and fellow Austrian émigré Leo Grillmair, for setting the bar for technical rock climbing and ski mountaineering in western Canada in the early 1950s.

Throughout the 1950s and '60s, Gmoser ran numerous ski-touring weeks to Stanley Mitchell Hut, pulling guests by snowmobile for the first 17 kilometres (10.5 miles) to Laughing Falls. In 1961, Gmoser and Grillmair built a new stone foundation for the hut and replaced the aging roof with a new metal one. In 1964, they enlisted three keen young Calgary skiers – Don Gardner, Gerry Walsh and Chic Scott – to transport a new stove to the hut, which they accomplished by stripping the thing of all its plates, bolts and doors and tying the shell to a pack frame.

"Hans and Leo took turns carrying the frame on their backs; it had to weigh 150 pounds," Scott recalled decades later. "That night, when myself and Donnie and Gerry went to bed – we were seventeen, eighteen – we listened to Hans play the zither, and Hans and Leo yodelling."

On one bluebird day, our group skied to Kiwetinok Pass and soaked in the view of countless unnamed snowy peaks rising like whitecaps on an ocean all the way to the horizon. The next day we savoured five yo-yo runs in perfectly spaced glades on the lower north-facing slopes of the Vice President.

Then, before embarking on what would be a smooth six-hour ski out to the highway, we soaked in the ambience of the hut on the last evening of our three-night stay. Lounging by the woodstove in one of the hut's well-worn, wooden-backed armchairs, I watched the logs crackle and glow behind the tinted glass door of the woodstove through a screen of steam rising from my mug of tea. I could almost hear a zither.

Chris Dodson, left, and Beth Dauk relax by the warmth of the woodstove in the Alpine Club of Canada's Stanley Mitchell Hut after a full day of backcountry skiing.

Best seasons: Like so many Rockies backcountry destinations, Little Yoho Valley is a treasure chest of alpine wonders in summer and winter, but with Yoho Valley Road closed to vehicles in the winter, the approach to Stanley Mitchell Hut, which in summer is 9.5 kilometres (6 miles) on a well-travelled trail, becomes a serious 23-kilometre (14-mile) backcountry ski tour. In summertime the utterly spectacular Takakkaw Falls, at 384 metres (1,260 feet) the second-highest waterfall in all of Canada, and accessible by car, is hands-down one of the most drop-dead unforgettable sights in the Rockies. To book a night at Whiskey Jack Hostel, visit www.hihostels.ca. To stay at the historic and charming Twin Falls Chalet, check out www.field.ca. For campsite information, visit www.pc.gc.ca.

Trailhead: From the Trans-Canada Highway, turn east onto Yoho Valley Road 3.7 kilometres (2.3 miles) east of Field, BC. Because of some VERY tight switchbacks, vehicles towing another unit cannot travel this road. Drive 13 kilometres (8 miles) to the large parking lot at the end of the road. Topo maps *Lake Louise 82 N/8, Blaeberry River 82 N/10.*

Takakkaw Falls Campground. This walk-in campground is one of the Rockies' great family destinations. Open mid-June to the end of September, the campground features spacious sites complete with fire rings, picnic tables, bear-proof food storage, a kitchen shelter and spectacular views beside a rushing creek. Better still, the 300-metre (984-foot) approach from your car is made easier with large, wheelbarrow-style carts to carry all your gear.

Laughing Falls, 4.2 kilometres (2.6 miles), 95 metres (312 feet) elevation gain, high point 1615 metres (5,299 feet), day hike or overnight.

   With several side trails to viewpoints along the way, there is hardly a better spot in the Rockies for a day hike with small kids or an overnight trip for first-time backpackers. And when you walk up close to the waterfall and feel its spray on your face, you'll know how the falls got its name.

Little Yoho Valley, 9.5 kilometres (6 miles), 555 metres (1,821 feet) elevation gain, high point 2075 metres (6,808 feet).

   This high alpine valley at the base of the glaciated President and Vice President peaks is the ideal destination for a first-time stay in a backcountry hut: www.alpineclubofcanada.ca. Just another 500 metres (550 yards) down the trail, Little Yoho Campground offers a charming spot to pitch your tent by a bubbling creek.

Iceline Trail, 11 kilometres (7 miles), 730 metres (2,395 feet) elevation gain, high point 2230 metres (7,316 feet).

   This slightly longer and steeper route to the Little Yoho Valley is the most scenic, well-graded hiking trail in Yoho National Park, along which you'll walk right past some small remnant glaciers and the magical aqua pools at their bases. Or, if it's a sunny day, lace up your trail shoes and take in the most scenic 20-kilometre (12.4-mile), full-day hike in the Rockies, returning via Celestine Lake and Laughing Falls.

Bust a Lung!

The President, 3138 metres (10,295 feet) and Vice President, 3066 metres (10,059 feet), A2.

With a hut and a campground right at their base, these two peaks are among the most popular classic mountaineering objectives in the Rockies. And the view from their summits, including the massive des Poilus Glacier to the east and Emerald Lake far below, isn't bad either.

Rock climbing: Takakkaw Falls, 5.6, seven pitches, 250 metres (820 feet).

Experienced trad climbers will not want to miss one of the most unique routes in the Rockies, which finishes with a full 60-metre (197-foot) belly crawl through a cave on the last pitch. The thundering of the waterfall will ring in your ears for days to come. For route info, visit www.rockclimbing.com.

Ice climbing: Takakkaw Falls, 250 metres (820 feet), V, WI4.

A serious test piece when it was first climbed in the 1970s, this Rockies classic is worth the 14-kilometre (8.7-mile) ski approach. See *Waterfall Ice: Climbs in the Canadian Rockies*, by Joe Josephson.

Ski mountaineering: Mount Field, 16 kilometres (10 miles) return, 1,300 metres (4265 feet) elevation gain, high point 2635 metres (8,645 feet).

Accessed by skiing up Yoho Valley Road for about 5 kilometres (3 miles), this very long climb is rewarded by a terrific view and a thigh-burning run down, both of which will keep you smiling for days. This is a big avalanche slope, however, which should only be attempted by experienced ski mountaineers when conditions are safe. See *Summits & Icefields: Alpine Ski Tours in the Canadian Rockies*, by Chic Scott.

Hire a guide: If you don't have the requisite skills and experience, hire a guide to take you on any of these adventures or to organize a custom trip: www.acmg.ca, www.yamnuska.com or www.internationalguidebureau.com.

Campbell Icefield Retirement Plan

Not long after he earned his pilot's licence in 1986, Bernie Schiesser began flying his Piper Arrow over the Rockies' jagged peaks, glacier-fed lakes and spruce-choked valleys. Eventually he found what he was looking for: a high alpine meadow set among rocky summits and shimmering glaciers, only 40 kilometres (25 miles) north of his home in Golden, BC. That spot, he decided, was the ideal location for a backcountry ski lodge.

"I flew up and down the mountains for days," Schiesser recalled. "And every year the snow was never out of there before July. You could ski right to the front door."

As soon as there was a door. Then, when Schiesser and his long-time friend, Exshaw resident Eric Lomas, learned that Parks Canada wanted to remove the Alpine Club of Canada's Freshfield Glacier Hut – which Schiesser and Lomas had built in the mid-1980s – they asked if they could have the building.

They dismantled the barely broken-in, five-year-old modular structure and flew it in sections by helicopter over the Continental Divide to a meadow near the Campbell Icefield. The hut remained in pieces, stacked under a tarp, for three years while they waited out the BC government's moratorium on new recreational backcountry licences. When the moratorium was

Campbell Icefield Chalet

lifted, they climbed a mountain of paperwork to secure their licence for winter backcountry use.

After reassembling the rudimentary shelter, they invited a few friends to go skiing. Then, after launching an ambitious construction project, they built a new, three-storey lodge, keeping the original building to use as overflow accommodation for staff and friends. In January 2003, they proudly opened their Campbell Icefield Chalet.

The ten-minute helicopter taxi took us over sparkling white slopes and rime-plastered rock faces, landing us in a field of snow 50 metres (164 feet) from the chalet's front door. When I stepped out of the helicopter, I could barely see the building at all from behind thigh-deep snowbanks. After unloading boxes of food and piles of gear, which we ferried to the front door by wooden toboggan, I watched the helicopter cruise into the twilight sky, leaving me feeling a bit like a castaway stranded on a desert isle. Our group of fifteen, however, was likely the most willing group of castaways ever abandoned by modern transportation, and I was fairly certain that when the chopper returned a week later to retrieve us, it would be far too soon.

LOCALS' LORE: *Eric Lomas is a founding member of the Association of Canadian Mountain Guides, the first non-European member to be invited into the International Federation of Mountain Guides Association, which oversees professional mountain guiding standards and training practices the world over. Formed in 1963, the ACMG now boasts more than 600 members. Bernie Schiesser became a member when he earned his guide's certification in 1967. Visit www.acmg.ca.*

Barely two hours after arriving, we'd already performed the compulsory avalanche transceiver and rescue practice. With synthetic skins applied to our ski bases, we snaked along single-file for a twenty-minute climb to the top of a tree-scattered slope for our first fresh tracks, making smooth turns in icing-sugar-soft powder right back to the chalet in time for dinner.

By morning, we'd contentedly embraced the lodge routine. Wake at first light, squirm into long underwear and mid-weight layers, sidle onto handmade pine benches at the dining tables, devour a home-cooked breakfast worthy of a farmhand, pack a Homer-Simpson-sized lunch including oven-warm cookies, fill the Thermos and daypack, throw on the outer layers, step into the skis and start working off breakfast. After skinning up and skiing down different untracked slopes all day, we'd relax in the wood-burning sauna before a hearty home-cooked dinner, and lounge in the living area before collapsing into bed. By the third morning I couldn't – and didn't want to – remember spending my days any other way.

There are about three dozen privately owned backcountry lodges scattered about the BC Rockies, Selkirk and Purcell mountain ranges where, like the Campbell chalet, guests are ferried in and out by a helicopter that does not return until the end of their usually week-long stay. The skiers spend their days climbing with skins through sparse forests or winding a trail through a crevasse field on a glacier bed, listening only to the wind and the squeak of their bindings. Then, after climbing for two, three or five hours, skiers peel off their skins and embrace the long run back to the lodge – or to the next climb for another run.

Ours was such a group: Randy, an Association of Canadian Mountain Guides (ACMG) assistant ski guide from Golden; Jesse, an aspiring ski guide from Banff; six Americans from New York, Idaho, Oregon and Washington State; five longtime Canmore residents; plus Schiesser plus Lomas's wife, Dorle, who would spoil us with her well-honed culinary talents for seven memorable days.

One day we skied four knee-deep runs near the chalet before returning for lunch, then headed back out for two more runs on higher, open slopes in the afternoon. Another day, we packed sandwiches and pastries and skied for three hours onto the Campbell Icefield only to retreat from advancing clouds and then spent the afternoon making multiple perfect spring-powder runs after the sun returned. One day, five of us skied in marginal light across the Campbell Icefield and halfway up an icefall on silhouetted Prior Peak some 10 kilometres (6 miles) and five hours from the chalet while more snow softly fell all around us.

Another day, I savoured the panorama of peaks from the top of the Bluewater Glacier and began to fully appreciate the countless ski possibilities – glades, open bowls and sprawling glaciers, all accessible as day tours from the chalet.

After dinner we shared conversation, celebrating what we didn't have – television, Internet and cell phones – dealing out playing cards as someone strummed Neil Young tunes on a guitar. Even though most of us were strangers at the week's start, we shared a fundamental camaraderie, a common language of basic ski modes, untouched landscapes, personal philosophies and, quite often, political ideologies too. The US had kicked off its war on Iraq that week, but without any

Bernie Schiesser demonstrates his classic style near the Campbell Icefield Chalet.

CHIC SCOTT

six o'clock news to inform us, we savoured a shared, contented, temporary obliviousness.

With eight decades' experience as certified mountain guides between them, Schiesser and Lomas recognize the goods. In 1955 Schiesser worked avalanche control in Rogers Pass, BC, with legendary Rockies guide Bruno Engler. Nearly a decade before that section of the Trans-Canada Highway would be built, Rogers Pass was accessible only by rail. Schiesser ran High Horizons Mountaineering Camp for teenagers for thirteen years, skiing on the Robertson Glacier in Kananaskis Country, and also served as president of the ACMG for seven years.

Originally from England, Lomas arrived in Banff in 1957 and operated the Banff Climbing School with former Banff National Park alpine specialist Peter Fuhrmann in the early 1960s before taking an avalanche control job in Stewart, BC.

"That was the toughest avalanche control in the western hemisphere," Lomas recalled. "There was 26 miles (42 kilometres) of road alongside a mountain where the snow slides all the time. We introduced the avalauncher. I was probably the first civilian in Canada to use artillery for avalanche control."

The two mountain men met in 1962 while working avalanche control for Parks Canada at the Lake Louise ski area. Lomas returned to Banff in 1980 and began guiding and teaching avalanche safety courses with Schiesser. Together they built the Alpine Club of Canada huts Peter and Catharine Whyte (Peyto), Lloyd MacKay (Mount Alberta), Neil Colgan and Scott Duncan. While skiing from the latter to the Trans-Canada Highway via Sherbrooke Lake, they were the first to take the most commonly used route today, the Schiesser/Lomas route. While constructing the Neil Colgan hut high above Moraine Lake on the Banff/Kootenay park boundary they also collaborated to establish the Schiesser Ledges access route.

And in the summer of 2001 they built the foundation and main structure of their three-storey, ten-bedroom chalet with the help of several Bow Valley carpenters, including Lomas's son André. The pine interior was put together the following summer and some finish work was completed in January 2003, two days before the season's first skiers arrived. With plenty of work still to be done, Lomas said he'd only skied about thirty days over the season.

"There's always something," Lomas said. "I just went out on the nice days."

After spending four weeks apiece at the chalet over the winter, both Schiesser and Lomas scoff at the idea of retiring.

"Yeah, it's a retirement plan, all right," Lomas said with a laugh. "A few years ago if anybody had said, 'You know what you're going to be doing when you're 71?' I'd have said 'No, and not this!' But it keeps you going. I think the longer you stay active, the better."

Schiesser agreed. "What is retirement?" he asked. "[The chalet is] just one more project, what the heck. Retiring is for those who want to retire."

Best season: Ski season at the Campbell Icefield Chalet operates from late December to early May, with frequent snowfalls providing plenty of fresh powder turns. Hire a guide or organize your own self-guided group. http://skigolden.com/index.htm

Trailhead: Accessed by helicopter only. The 10-minute flight is staged out of Donald, a 30-minute drive west from Golden, BC. Topo maps *Blaeberry River 82 N/10, Bluewater 82 N/11*.

The chalet's ten bedrooms accommodate up to 22 guests, complete with indoor night toilet, running cold water and my favourite sauna/shower room setup of any backcountry touring lodge. And the area's terrain makes it an ideal getaway for backcountry skiers of all levels in guided or self-guided groups.

Mount Alan Campbell, 3030 metres (9,941 feet).

If you've got the legs, lungs and avalanche safety and route-finding skills, the ski up Mount Alan Campbell will reward you with stunning views of countless Rocky and Selkirk peaks, including 3612-metre (11,850-foot) Mount Forbes. Or for a truly rewarding big day tour, ascend East Peak, then drop down the north-facing glacier toward the Valenciennes River and return to the chalet via the High Col. Maps *Blaeberry River 82 N/10, Bluewater 82 N/11*. For info on BC's other backcountry lodges, visit www.backcountrylodg-esofbc.com.

Hire a guide: If you don't have the requisite skills and experience, hire a guide to take you on any of these adventures or to organize a custom trip: www.acmg.ca, www.yamnuska.com or www.internationalguidebureau.com.

Seven Slopes in Seven Days

The wind was everywhere, a brutal, tangible force pushing from all sides. With my head shielded by my jacket hood, I fixed my eyes on the ski tails a few metres ahead, but the wind erased their tracks like a vigorously shaken Etch-a-Sketch. A cliff-bound face loomed in front of me through a swirl of cloud and then it was gone, as if someone switched a remote control back to a screen of churning wind and snow. On previous trips I had simply focused on reaching the destination – a hut, a vehicle or even home. This time, the destination was whatever place we stopped to set up camp. There and here were the same.

DAY ONE

Tony told Brian he thought the pinwheels of soft snow rolling down the walls of the canyon on our way up to Bow Hut looked like cinnamon buns. Brian had met Tony eight years earlier at Hudson Bay Mountain in Smithers, BC, and they'd been day-touring buddies ever since. I had winter camped once, below treeline, with a campfire. Camping on the glacier en route from Bow Hut, on the eastern edge of the Wapta Icefield, to Stanley Mitchell Hut in the Little Yoho Valley, would be a first for all three of us.

As the only woman with seven men – all of them strangers to me except our camp manager, John – I was determined not to be the slowest, so I was relieved to learn Jim had never skied with a pack or away from groomed slopes before. In fact, a groomed run was where he'd tested his brand new, lightweight pack, skis and boots. Dave was a law professor from Tempe, Arizona, whose disco-era touring gear was the exact opposite of Jim's, his antique boots consisting of black plastic shells with red wire bales that hooked onto wedges protruding from the shells like cauliflower ears. Nylon gaiters attached to the boots by Velcro and his cumbersome Head skis had no sidecut or camber. Less than two hours into our first day, John was dressing Dave's blisters.

After a quick run on the glacier, John served up a hearty pasta dinner with wine and I quickly decided I liked the fact our food had been carried up to the hut by porters. Afterward I asked Dave why he'd joined this fully guided and catered Alpine Club of Canada (ACC)-organized trip.

"It's easier than doing it yourself. It takes so much work to figure out the food," Dave said. "This way you get here and somebody lights the fire for you. It's the lap of luxury on the glacier."

DAY TWO

We skinned up the glacier like schoolchildren heading off on a field trip, passing half a dozen partially constructed igloos crumbling in the snow like ancient ruins obscured by blowing snow.

We aimed for Mount Rhondda's faint summit under a dull sky, snaking past broken-rock gullies that dropped down from the summit ridge into the nothingness of the glacier deck far below. We didn't linger on the summit, dutifully following our guide, Lars Andrews, downslope. Suddenly the clouds broke and we savoured 600 metres (1,968 feet) of fresh powdery turns in beaming sunshine. Looking back up at our tracks curving in the snow, two crevasses lurked on either side of our s-marks, their shadows sitting like a pair of sunglass lenses with our turns drawn between them down the bridge of a broad, flat nose.

After dinner we sipped from a plastic Coke bottle filled with fine port and a plastic salad dressing bottle containing single-malt scotch. Jim, a school headmaster from Baton Rouge, Louisiana, shaved his beard meticulously with a small electric razor at the common-room table as Brian, an accountant, downloaded the day's travel data from his altimeter watch. Jim told us how on his first ACC trip to Jasper's Fryatt Valley in 1972, he'd witnessed Canadian climbing pioneer Phyllis Munday slug an unco-operative horse. Ever the educator, Jim believed he too should keep learning.

"I was dying to adapt other experiences to the ski environment," he said. "Mount Rhondda, skiing off the glacier, doing a ski descent – that was all new. It was great!"

We listened intently as Lars served up pointers on winter camping. At thirty, Lars was already internationally certified through the Association of Canadian Mountain Guides (ACMG), but with his No Fear T-shirt, tousled blond hair busting out from under a ball cap, baggy black ski pants and silver-studded black belt with a red and black biker buckle, he looked more like a snowboarder, a rapper or maybe a BMXer, but not a traditional mountain guide.

DAY THREE

Lars set a slow and steady pace through flat light and blowing snow up the gradual slope above Bow Hut.

"My pack is heavy, too," he said encouragingly. "I don't like it either."

My pack was at least forty-five pounds, as I carried one-third of the food I would share with my tentmates, Brian and Tony, who each carried a little more than me. I started to feel a bit guilty about it but reminded myself I was at least eight inches shorter and at least forty pounds lighter than either of them. I didn't want any of the men to feel like they needed to look out for me, but at the same time I appreciated it if they offered once in a while.

Backcountry skiers ascend the glacier headwall above the Alpine Club of Canada's Bow Hut, the Wapta Icefield's St. Nicholas Peak ahead.

Lars pulled out the rope, tying himself into one end, John into the other and Norbert, a grandfather from Germany, in the centre. Always smiling, Norbert had once skied for a week across Greenland. He had come to see the Canadian Rockies, but he wasn't seeing much of them that day. Above the icefall we stopped on a plateau at our intended campsite, from where we had hoped to climb to the summit of Mount Collie. Bracing against a monstrously fierce wind, we dug a patio-sized round pit and, using skis, poles and ice axes, staked a twisting and flapping tent fly securely to the ground over the trench. That done, we quickly huddled inside for lunch.

Back out in the storm, I quickly realized how comfortable and protected we'd been in our makeshift shelter. Moving along in a whiteout, Lars and John stopped every fifteen minutes to take compass and GPS readings, while all we could see was each other's clothing. We reached another steep climb with a steep drop down the far side. Lars skied down a bit and climbed back up, then asked Brian and Tony how they felt about sideslipping to the imperceptible bottom of the pitch. The two strongest skiers after Lars and John, they asked him how bad it was.

"Shit," Lars replied. "As bad as can be."

They shrugged and started down while Lars set up a belay on a rocky bench to lower the rest of us on the rope. Norbert and Jim descended slowly, their skis grating on the wind-blasted surface until they reached John waiting below.

"You're going to move down this quickly, right? You don't have anything to worry about, you're on the rope," Lars instructed Dave and me. "No problem," I replied. The surface was hard as marble, and even with the added weight of my pack, my edges wouldn't hold. I let my skis run, tugging on Dave who was tied into the rope a bit above me on the slope, stopping each time he fell.

Forcing our legs to make survival turns, we skied down the glacier, the light so flat I felt nauseous. John and Lars spent nearly an hour helping us ready our sites before pitching their own tent, and by dusk Tony was sitting in our vestibule boiling snow for our freeze-dried dinners. After the commotion of Bow Hut, we felt somewhat isolated as the wind engulfed any sound from the other two tents.

"We're in our pods now," Tony said.

DAY FOUR

I had skied the standard Wapta Traverse once before, spending nights at Peter and Catharine Whyte (Peyto), Rob Ritchie (Balfour) and Scott Duncan huts, blessed with warm and sunny spring days. That was how I had envisioned camping on the glacier, sipping tea and admiring the stars and the view. Counting on the same vision, Tony had shivered all night in a summer-weight sleeping bag. Super fit, he'd competed in the Canadian Ironman the previous summer.

"I've always wanted to do a traverse," Tony told me. "It appeals to me to move across snow, not just stay in one hut. But camping was the challenge. I was wet."

Christina Brodribb skins up the Vulture Glacier in one of the Wapta Icefield's frequent whiteouts en route between the Alpine Club of Canada's Rob Ritchie (Balfour) and Bow huts.

Brian started the stove for us to have tea and oatmeal. Slow to leave my toasty –40°c-rated (–40°F) bag, I felt guilty because I didn't leap to start the stove first. Fine snow filled every possible corner of our packs and boot shells, pots and food bags in the tent's back and front vestibules. I dreaded shoving my feet into my cold boot liners and decided I didn't love winter camping.

Lars ducked under our tent fly, a toothbrush in his mouth. Via satellite phone he'd learned the weather was expected to improve that afternoon, then worsen by nightfall. We wouldn't climb Mount des Poilus that day; we'd ski straight to Stanley Mitchell Hut. I didn't state aloud how that had been my wish all along, but I felt better that Tony and Brian weren't objecting either.

Soon we we'd packed up and returned to our routine of skinning up, grabbing a bite and moving on, which had become just that: a comfortable routine. We'd evolved into a nomadic band of skiers, travelling as a unit.

Less than an hour into our day's travel we looked up toward Isolated Col, a very steep, narrow notch between rocky peaks. Lars explained the options of going that way or the longer but gentler route around the Whaleback.

"That looks like fun," Tony said, eyeing the col.

"I hope we go the other way," Norbert replied.

Lars decided the col presented too many potential hazards with slow-moving skiers laden with heavy packs. We'd go around the Whaleback. I was disappointed and relieved at the same time. Not long afterward we heard a rumble and watched an avalanche tumble down east-facing cliffs.

"I guess we made the right decision," Lars commented casually.

The ascent around the Whaleback was slow and laborious. My pack felt heavy, my skis felt heavy, my legs felt heavy, even the snowflakes clinging to my toque felt heavy. I lagged behind. I was tired, admitting it out loud to John.

"Everyone's getting tired," he assured me. Then it got hard.

Lars led us down into a steep, narrow gully that would eventually drop us down onto the trail to the hut.

I traversed, made a kick-turn, traversed, another kick-turn, lurching my way down the steep, narrow natural half-pipe. In search of a shortcut to the trail below, Tony and I followed Lars's track into the forest, ducking and twisting around tight trees and bushes. Our detour was fruitless.

Skiers apply climbing skins to their skis at Stanley Mitchell Hut in preparation for a day of skiing in Little Yoho Valley.

> **LOCALS' LORE:** *In March 2008, Canmore locals Will Gadd, Phil Villeneuve and Graham Maclean skied the entire Wapta Traverse, from Peyto Lake to Sherbrooke Lake in eight furiously fast hours. Using lightweight touring skis they each carried a small pack with the bare minimum to keep them alive should they be caught out by a sudden storm. They climbed 1500 metres (4,921 feet) and made 1810 metres (5,938 feet) of downhill turns.*

"Abort mission!" After bushwhacking plenty of times with my friends, it was gratifying to know guides sometimes do it too.

"My dad used to take me through crap like this all the time and call it 'ski touring'," Lars said. I suggested perhaps that's what prompted him to become a guide: so he could tell his dad where to go.

We arrived at Stanley Mitchell Hut a day early, imposing somewhat on a group of ten who weren't set to leave until the next morning. I missed the solitude of the glacier already, but as I curled up in an armchair beside the crackling woodstove while John gently strummed the hut guitar, I was completely and utterly content.

DAY FIVE

We skied up toward the President Glacier, into a forceful wind. I could barely remember any other way to start the day, but a big part of me wanted to be sipping tea by the woodstove. We pushed forward determinedly, the wind slamming into our faces.

"Can we camp here?" Jim asked jokingly. "We know how."

We were being pummelled, beaten by a nasty snowstorm, but we were laughing. We'd gelled, we'd become cohesive layers of our own snowpack. We retreated, skied down the moraine, then headed west toward Kiwetinok Pass. Wrong way. The wind chased us back to the hut in record time.

The spontaneous work party was exactly what I needed. John enthusiastically led the crew, some men shovelling the roof, Tony chopping wood. Dave dried out his gear while I happily sought out indoor chores, cleaning the stovetop and sweeping the sleeping rooms.

After a hot lunch, we headed to the glades on the lower slopes of the Vice President. At the top of our second run through heavenly, fluffy, knee-deep powder planted with perfectly spaced trees, Tony and Brian insisted Norbert go first.

"This is our backyard, we do this all the time," Brian said. "You don't get to do this in Germany."

Norbert was unsure. "Where do I go?"

"Down, just down!"

"But where?" Finally Norbert was persuaded to grab first tracks, while Brian, Tony, John and I embraced the familiar yo-yo routine of skinning up, skiing down.

The forest was calm; the sun shone for our fourth and final run. Norbert broke into song, rendering Beethoven's *Ode to Joy* in full and deep German as John played air violin with his ski poles.

DAY SIX

As we reached the previous day's turn-around point on the moraine, Norbert announced he didn't feel up to a climb. His arm was sore and stiff. We pleaded with him but his mind was made up; he would join Jim who was nursing a sore calf at the hut.

Lars was noticeably disappointed. "I know he'd do really well."

The glacier surface was wind-scoured, with ridges and ripples like meringue frozen solid. Lars skied directly up the President Glacier. At the snow-filled bergschrund he laid his skis horizontally in front of him on the nearly vertical slope and started kicking steps. At the top of the 20-metre (66-foot) wall he cut away the cornice for us to climb though to the col that connected the President and Vice President peaks.

With a chilly wind pushing up from the far side of the col above Emerald Glacier, we started toward the President's summit. Ski pole in one hand, ice axe in the other, I followed Brian on the rope, Tony behind me, then Dave, while John climbed solo.

Progress was intermittent: a dozen solid steps followed by two dozen lousy ones in sugary snow that had collected around the bases of discontinuous rock bands and had all the cohesiveness of desert sand. Stopping and starting kept my fingers painfully cold, and maybe it was because I'd already climbed the President one balmy summer morning a few years earlier that I silently decided I didn't love winter alpine climbing either. We had no view, but thankfully no sense of exposure either. Lars started up a 5-metre (16-foot) chimney but found the snow rotten, the footholds unstable.

"This is heinous, this is full on," he stated. Unwilling to surrender, he tried again to climb the chimney, but ultimately decided that even if he could coax all of us up the pitch, he wouldn't be able to build an anchor adequate for our descent. Our high point of 3083 metres (10,115 feet) was Brian's lifetime high point. Although he was in his mid-fifties, his fitness was exemplary; until then his biggest challenge on our trip had been escaping his office at tax time.

"I love this country, I love being out," Brian said. "Given good health and opportunity, if it means something to you, you'd better grab it now, not put it off."

The run back down was awful. In boot-deep, heavy and dense snow, my thighs screamed. Down, down, it mutated into breakable crust. Tough slab, cement crust, frozen and wind-sculpted patches, every metre descended worse than the last. Lars appeared to cruise along, as did Brian and John, while Tony cursed his telemark skis and I struggled to stay on my feet, resting frequently.

Dave was doomed. His arms swung in the air as he sped out of control and crashed with the rhythm of a rock 'em sock 'em boxer, as John followed patiently behind to retrieve lost pieces of gear and help Dave back onto his feet. Dave never uttered a single complaint.

"Dave, you're like Rocky Balboa, you just keep getting up off the mat," Lars cried. We divided the contents of Dave's pack among us, including the pack, finally reaching the lower slopes of the moraine and cutting Dave's number of falls per metre descended by at least half. Near the bottom of our miserable run, a 3-metre (10-foot) section of bare rock separated us from the only decent four turns the day would offer.

"If you like your skis you might want to carry them over this stuff," Lars suggested, pointing to the limestone slab. But to Dave he shrugged, "Dave, you just walk those Heads all over that shit."

Earlier, John had remarked how it was refreshing to see someone who hadn't fully succumbed to competitive gear acquisition.

"What you lack in gear you make up for in attitude," John congratulated Dave.

DAY SEVEN

I hit the trail first, my skis gliding silently in 10 centimetres (4 inches) of light, fluffy powder, the trail offering just enough decline that I was able to coast, my usually squeaky boots not breaking the 7 a.m. quiet. While the fresh snow made the tight switchback descent to Laughing Falls relatively smooth, later on all except Lars struggled with a bad wax day on the 13-kilometre (8-mile) Takakkaw Falls road, where up to 20 centimetres (8 inches) of sticky snow clung stubbornly to our ski bases.

"I haven't noticed," Lars shrugged. "I'm just givin' 'er."

"That's what we're doing wrong, we just have to give 'er," I suggested with a laugh.

After a week in the Canadian Rockies, even Norbert understood the Canadian lingo, and with a little glide wax on our bases, we did just that all the way to the parking lot.

Maybe next time I would camp for two nights.

AUTHOR'S NOTE: *A couple of years later I did winter camp two consecutive nights at Bostock Creek in Glacier National Park in BC's Selkirks. We pitched our tent right at treeline, and with the temperature never dropping below –15°C (5°F), it was a reasonably pleasant experience. Away from the more populated slopes closer to Rogers Pass's cozy huts, the skiing in untracked powder was spectacular.*

Best seasons: While the Wapta Icefield is the Rockies' premier ski trav\
and ski-mountaineering destination, the area is also an excellent playgrou\
for summer mountaineering adventures. For a special treat from mid-May to mid-October, spend a night in the 1920s-era art-deco-inspired living museum Num-Ti-Jah Lodge, right on the shores of brilliant turquoise Bow Lake: www.num-ti-jah.com. To book a spot in one of the Alpine Club of Canada's four Wapta Icefield huts, visit www.alpineclubofcanada.ca/facility.

Trailhead: From the Trans-Canada Highway, exit onto the Icefields Parkway, Highway 93 North. Drive for 36 kilometres (22.4 miles) and turn left onto the Num-Ti-Jah Lodge access road. Park in the big lot just before you reach the lodge. Topo maps *Hector Lake 82 N/9*, *Golden 82 N/7*, *Lake Louise 82 N/8*, *Blaeberry River 82 N/10*.

Bow Lake shoreline hike, 1.5 kilometres (1 mile) one-way, no elevation gain, high point 1950 metres (6,400 feet).

This stunning turquoise, glacier-fed lake is without a doubt one of the most inviting spots in the Rockies for a picnic or for a leisurely stroll on the well-graded trail that hugs its shoreline. Bring binoculars and you can see Bow Hut perched up high below the leaning spire of Saint Nicholas Peak right at the edge of the glacier.

Snowshoeing or cross-country skiing: In winter, bring your cross-country skis or snowshoes and walk right across the frozen lake.

Bow Glacier Falls, 4.6 kilometres (3 miles), 155 metres (500 feet) elevation gain, high point 2105 metres (6,900 feet).

In summer, hike the shoreline trail up beyond a natural bridge created by a massive chockstone firmly wedged between the canyon walls above the gushing torrent. Continue to the main outwash area below Bow Glacier Falls, the headwaters of the Bow River and the South Saskatchewan River system.

Bow Hut, 8 kilometres (5 miles), 390 metres (1,280 feet) elevation gain, high point 2330 metres (7,644 feet).

In summer, this hike involves a couple of unbridged river crossings higher up the valley which could be problematic early in the season when the water is at its highest due to snowmelt. By mid- to late-July, however, access to this alpine hut is straightforward hiking on a high alpine trail. Spend a night high above treeline and explore just beyond the hut to discover a cluster of tiny ponds set in the moraine. Scrambling up the Onion Skin, the broad, rounded summit northwest of the hut can be accomplished without stepping on the glacier. DO NOT venture onto the glacier without a rope and harnesses and crevasse rescue skills.

Wapta Traverse, Peyto Lake to Sherbrooke Lake, 39 kilometres (24 miles), 1500 metres (4,921 feet) elevation gain, high point 2930 metres (9,613).

This classic Rockies traverse traditionally involves overnight stays at the ACC huts Peter and Catharine Whyte (Peyto), Rob Ritchie (Balfour) and Scott Duncan. From each of these huts, if you've got the time and good weather, you can bag a number of peaks, including mounts Baker, Olive, and Balfour and Saint Nicholas Peak.

Alternatively, if you're keen on camping on a glacier, consider the 20-kilometre (12.4-mile) Bow–Yoho traverse from Bow Hut to Stanley Mitchell Hut in Little Yoho Valley, and climb mounts Collie and des Poilus along the way. See *Summits & Icefields: Alpine Ski Tours in the Canadian Rockies*, by Chic Scott. Check out www. alpineclubofcanada.ca/activities to join a guided ACC adventure.

Ice climbing: Bow Falls, 95 metres (312 feet) III, WI3–4.

This classic ice climb tends to form early and fat. It presents minimal avalanche hazard and provides a day spent in a fabulous alpine wilderness setting. See Joe Josephson's book *Waterfall Ice: Climbs in the Canadian Rockies*.

Hire a guide: If you don't have the requisite skills and experience, hire a guide to take you on any of these adventures or to organize a custom trip: www.acmg.ca, www.yamnuska.com, www.internationalguidebureau.com or http://rockies-ice.com.

10

Willingdon Adventure Reveals Rockies' Exquisite Corner

Among the hundreds of mountains that comprise the Canadian Rockies, fifty-four (and by some measures one or two more) reach above 11,000 feet, or 3353 metres. The highest is Mount Robson, which, at 3954 metres (12,972 feet), is a massive block of a mountain that rises a full 200 metres (656 feet) above its nearest rival in stature, 3747-metre (12,293-foot) Mount Columbia. Both are big, glaciated mountains that require climbers to have experience in glacier travel and roped mountaineering techniques to negotiate their complicated high-alpine terrain.

While Colorado has its 14ers – an equal number of mountains that reach above 14,000 feet (4268 metres) – not one of those comes even close to boasting Robson's world-class 3000-metre (9,843-foot) base-to-summit vertical elevation. And while a couple of the Canadian Rockies 11,000ers can be climbed in an average day without ropes, barely a handful do not require overnights in the backcountry. Rather, most require several days to accommodate the drive from the nearest town, the approach hike and the actual climbing of the mountain – not to mention the crucial safe snow and ice conditions, good weather and suitably experienced, skilled partners. While the quickest person to climb all of the Colorado 14ers took only sixteen days, the fastest time of any of the half-dozen people who have climbed all fifty-four Canadian Rockies 11,000ers goes to Canmore's Nancy Hansen, who completed her goal in 2003 in an impressively speedy seven years and forty-nine days.

Given that the 11,000ers include such notoriously loose, crumbly and downright terrifying peaks as the North, South and Centre Goodsirs and Mount Alberta – which is nonetheless a stunning form to behold from the charming little six-person Alpine Club of Canada Lloyd MacKay Hut at its base – climbing the 11,000ers is definitely not on my bucket list.

Exploring new (to me, at least) corners of the Canadian Rockies, especially those that boast one of the 11,000ers' most beautiful bivy spots (as recommended in Bill Corbett's guidebook *The 11,000ers of the Canadian Rockies*), does, however, constitute one of my more passionate reasons for breathing. The fact that 3373-metre (11,066-foot) Mount Willingdon, one of the least known of the fifty-four 11,000ers, is an easy climb, mostly a scramble with a tricky bit just below the summit, made it extra enticing to me.

Indeed, from a climber's perspective, Mount Willingdon is so unremarkable that the first ascent party of surveyors who climbed its rubbly slopes while working on the 1919 Dominion Boundary Survey didn't bother to tell anyone about it. Evidence of their ascent left on the summit was the cause of much chagrin for Osgood Field, who led a climbing party to the mountain six years later in hopes of nabbing a first ascent of an 11,000er.

Though not a first ascent, nor a difficult one, my trip up Mount Willingdon with two friends in the summer of 2009 delivered many rewards. The off-trail hike over 2590-metre (8,500-foot) Quartzite Col laden with multi-day packs did indeed make the approach almost as big as the climb, taking the slowest member of our party nearly eleven hours to reach our campsite near the shore of the lovely and largest of the three vibrantly blue Devon Lakes. From Quartzite Col,

Livia Hrehova hikes up the final stretch to Mount Willingdon's summit.

the view looking north down the Siffleur River valley was spectacular, not to mention fascinating when I thought about how it formed a section of one of the Rockies' oldest and best-travelled early routes. As described in Emerson Sanford and Janice Sanford Beck's *Life of the Trail 1* book, evidence shows that Native people were regularly journeying from Lake Louise to Kootenay Plains (now a natural area on the David Thompson Highway) long before James Hector became, in 1859, the first European to travel from the Bow River to the North Saskatchewan over Pipestone Pass, which divides the waters flowing south to the Bow and north to the North Saskatchewan.

Branching off to the east from the Siffleur Valley, Clearwater Pass lured us over wide open hills of golden grass bathed in late-evening sun to meadows at the base of Mount Willingdon,

> **LOCALS' LORE:** *Devon Lakes (there are three) were stocked with brook trout in the 1960s, in hopes of luring anglers to the area. Before long, however, the non-native brook trout began to disrupt the natural ecosystem, not just of the lakes but of the surrounding rivers too, as they crowded out native species such as the bull trout. In 2003, Parks Canada staff removed more than 2,000 brook trout from the Devon Lakes and also the Upper Clearwater River. Through these actions Parks biologists hope to return the lakes to their natural state.*

which bursts into the sky alongside neighbouring mounts Crown and Willingdon 3. The area is so lovely it enticed renowned paleontologist Charles Walcott and his wife, Mary Vaux Walcott, to spend more than two weeks there in 1920. No doubt searching for fossils, Walcott, who is credited with the discovery of the Burgess Shale, now a UNESCO World Heritage Site in Yoho National Park, would likely have hiked up easy terrain to the giant crown of rock halfway up Willingdon. It was there that nearly ninety years later we marvelled at walls of honeycombed quartzite perched atop a bed of fine, white South Pacific-quality sand, a little island of maritime wonder amid the comparatively plain, dark-grey limestone of the slopes above and below it.

After surmounting a short but steep and thankfully multi-pocketed wall to reach its final rubbly slopes, we stood on Willingdon's summit, where the register, bearing the names of only one or two parties in the busiest of summers, reminded us of the remoteness of our adventure.

As we were tucked into our tents that night – the only tents in sight – the thunderstorms booming around us reminded us of just that solitude. Thankfully, we woke to clear blue skies, which stayed with us throughout our two-day hike out, most of it above treeline, over Pipestone Pass to Fish Lakes and over North Molar Pass back to the Mosquito Creek trailhead.

Climbers' tents sit in a tranquil alpine meadow below Mount Willingdon in Banff's Clearwater Valley.

I savoured those final steps before the dirt trail intersected the pavement of the Icefields Parkway, happy not only to have bagged a Rockies 11,000er but also to have explored another of this range's exquisitely magical corners.

Best seasons: Summer is definitely the best for hiking and scrambling in the Mosquito Creek, Fish Lakes, Pipestone Pass and Mount Willingdon area. Backcountry skiers, however, will enjoy a pleasant tour up Mosquito Creek to North Molar Pass. Be sure to acquire a backcountry camping permit before setting out, by calling the Lake Louise Parks Information Centre at 403.522.3833.

Trailhead: The Mosquito Creek trailhead is located at the north end of the bridge on the east side of the Icefields Parkway, 24 kilometres (15 miles) north of the Trans-Canada Highway interchange. Park at the Mosquito Creek

Hostel lot on the west side of the road, at the south end of the bridge. Topo maps *Hector Lake 82 N/9, Siffleur River 82 N/16*.

Family Friendly

Spend a night – or two or three – at the rustic and charming HI-Mosquito Creek Wilderness Hostel. With dorm-style or simple private rooms, this off-the-grid hostel offers warm comfort in a real wilderness setting. Cook in the fully equipped kitchen, relax in the wood-burning sauna or curl up by the fireplace. With a rushing creek nearby in summer or deep snowbanks in winter, the woods outside the door offer an outdoor paradise for any kid's imagination. Visit www.hihostels.ca.

Sweat a Little

North Molar Pass, 11.5 kilometres (7 miles), 760 metres elevation gain (2,493 feet), high point 2590 metres (8,497 feet).

By boot in summer or ski in winter, the route following Mosquito Creek leads to one of the most extensive alpine meadowlands in all of Banff National Park – and some enjoyable moderate-level ski turns in the winter.

Sweat a Lot

Upper Fish Lake backpack, 15 kilometres (9.3 miles), 760 metres (2,493 feet) elevation gain, 365 metres (1,198 feet) elevation loss, high point 2590 metres (8,500 feet).

From the summit of North Molar Pass it's downhill all the way to Upper Fish Lake campground, but since you'll be high above treeline for most of that distance, the views stretching in every direction will allow you to completely forget the weight of the camping gear on your back. Set up camp and continue on toward Pipestone Valley, following a trail that stays high and keeps your spirits there too.

Bust a Lung!

Mount Willingdon, 3373 metres (11,066 feet).

There's no getting around the fact that the approach to Mount Willingdon's base is a long hike, but then its very remoteness is one of the best reasons for visiting the area. For those comfortable and experienced in off-trail travel, the hike over Quartzite Col offers a

varied and rewarding approach. From the Mosquito Creek trailhead, follow the trail for 6.5 kilometres (4 miles) to a campsite, and then turn left (north) and follow small, unofficial trails alongside a creek (and sometimes upslope through forest). Head northeast up grassy slopes and aim up toward an amphitheatre littered with massive boulders, which leads to Quartzite Col. Viewed from the top of the col, the sheer size of the Siffleur River valley below will astonish you, and if the weather is good you'll see Willingdon looming unmistakably to the east. The hike over hummocky hills across the Siffleur River valley will take longer than you'll think it will, but keep heading east and you'll connect with a well-graded trail that will deliver you directly to Devon Lakes at Willingdon's base. Make sure to get a permit to camp there (available at the Lake Louise Parks Information Centre). The climb up Willingdon's west ridge is straightforward, with only a downsloping 5-metre-high (16-foot) cliffband forming the crux of the climb. For a detailed route description, check out *The 11,000ers of the Canadian Rockies*, by Bill Corbett.

Hire a guide: If you don't have the requisite skills and experience, hire a guide to take you on any of these adventures or to organize a custom trip: www.acmg.ca, www.yamnuska.com or www.internationalguidebureau.com.

11

Icefall Ski Tour Expands the Possible

The first time I skied at Icefall Lodge, in 2007, owner Larry Dolecki described a ski tour he had once done with some guests. They had skinned up from the lodge for about 1250 metres (4,100 feet), then skied down to valley bottom for 2150 metres (7,050 feet) of fresh turns before skinning back up another 900 metres (2,950 feet) to the lodge.

Sounds totally cool, I thought, but I immediately checked myself with "but that's too big for me." The Tempest Glacier tour was promptly shelved in the back of my mind alongside other mountain myths and adventures of superhuman proportions beyond my mere mortal grasp.

When I returned to Icefall Lodge two winters later, I fully appreciated five delightful moderate days, skinning up and skiing down 1200 vertical metres (3,940 feet) of untracked glaciers and steep, old-growth cedar forest runs each day. I also appreciated the comfort of the brand-new three-storey lodge, much larger than the original cabin, which now provides extra sleeping quarters.

Bordering Banff National Park on the western edge of the Canadian Rockies adjacent to the Lyells – five of the Rockies' peaks above 3,353 metres (11,000 feet) – Icefall's 200-square-kilometre (77-square-mile) tenure is a backcountry skier's nirvana. The largest of BC's ski-touring outfits, Icefall is located on the west

LOCALS' LORE: *The five distinct peaks of the Lyells, all of which soar above 3353 metres (11,000 feet) and together form the Mount Lyell massif, were individually named in 1972 in honour of five early Swiss mountain guides who settled in Golden, BC, and devoted their careers to guiding clients up peaks throughout the Canadian Rockies: Rudolph Aemmer (Peak 1), brothers Edward Jr. (2), Ernest (3) and Walter (4) Feuz (pronounced "foitz"), and Christian Häsler Jr. (5). Edouard Feuz Sr. and Christian Häsler Sr. were the first Swiss guides hired by Canadian Pacific in 1899, to be stationed at Glacier House in Glacier National Park (Rogers Pass). Glacier National Park in British Columbia, Canada, was designated in 1886; Glacier National National Park in Montana, US, was established in 1910.*

slope of the Rockies near the Continental Divide, which gives it a deep and stable snowpack, more like BC's Interior ranges such as the Selkirks (where many other backcountry touring and heli- and cat-skiing operations are located), and unlike most of the Rockies, where the snow is often shallow and poorly bonded.

After growing up in Calgary, Dolecki earned an economics degree from Queens University in Ontario in 1989. But a ski/snowboard sabbatical in the French Alps exposed him to the mountain guiding profession and soon lured him to pursue the arduous path of gaining international certification with the Association of Canadian Mountain Guides, which he completed in 1999.

With the experience of countless hut nights in Europe, as well as in BC's touring and heli-skiing lodges, Dolecki teamed up with Golden-based mountain guide Jim Gudjonson to build Icefall Lodge. They hosted their first skiers in 2006, and later that year, Dolecki assumed full ownership of the business. Skiers are flown to the lodge on Saturdays and don't see the helicopter again until the following weekend. They spend their days climbing up virgin mountain slopes, using gripping skins on their ski bases which they then remove for the big run back down. At the end of the day they feast on well-earned dinners prepared by talented cooks, relax in the wood-burning sauna and sleep soundly under toasty down duvets before waking up to do it all over again.

Our diverse group included one trio who were modelling for a sportswear catalogue: two skiers and a snowboarder touring on her splitboard (which separates for the climb up, then reattaches for the ride back down). Two photographers – one of them a first-time backcountry skier from Boston – plus two aspiring ski guides training under Dolecki's supervision completed our party. On our first day, Dolecki had instructed everyone in the group on the use of avalanche transceivers, probes and shovels, sharing key pointers for safe travel in avalanche terrain.

Every day, he broke trail for us to follow, sometimes through snow above his knees.

On the Thursday night, Dolecki prepared us for our final day. "Pack a headlamp and a good lunch. We'll leave at 8:30 a.m.," he instructed.

With light snow falling, we skinned up toward Kemmel Mountain, with Dolecki pushing a steadier pace than on previous days. Feeling tired after a full week of ski touring, I half wished for a full-blown storm so I could retreat to the sauna. I never asked exactly where we were going; I just resolutely pushed myself to follow. After two hours of climbing we stopped and peeled off our skins. Flat light provided extra excitement for an untracked glacier run down toward a valley adjacent to the one we'd climbed up. We couldn't see much, but at least the turns felt pretty good.

Then we regrouped for the next climb. "If the light stays like this," Dolecki said, pointing to silhouetted cliffbands looming above the monotone snowfield, "we'll climb all the way up that glacier for about two and a half hours."

I purposefully ate and drank, summoning all my energy and accepting the reality of a long day out.

Visibility was marginal, a few closer peaks barely winking

through the clouds. Then we rounded a corner on the moraine to face a giant jumble of séracs. Instantly, anticipation evaporated all my tiredness like spindrift off the rock walls. We were climbing through an icefall!

Weaving a safe line between a maze of crevasses and tottering sérac towers, Dolecki led us past glacial formations that revealed tunnels and caves. Skiing slowly uphill in the snowy quiet, I felt like we were clandestinely investigating an unknown planet.

Then, from a snowy bulge on the slope, surrounded by silhouetted jagged cliffs and glimmering blue ice blocks, we stripped off our skins for the long, 1500-metre-plus (5,000-foot) run down.

But first, Dolecki skied a short distance down around a roll and stopped at the mouth of a slot canyon cleaved into the glacier. "I think we can ski through here – follow me," he motioned.

Tingling with anticipation, we peered into a hole that dropped five metres (16.5 feet) below the glacier's surface. Dolecki skied down into the passageway where 15-metre (49-foot) walls of striated blue ice towered above him. Then, with Corin, one of the practicum guides, belaying him on a rope and the rest of us holding our breath, Dolecki disappeared through the ice corridor. After a distant shout from Dolecki, Corin followed. Yippee, they'd made it through, the canyon was clear!

With giant butterflies fluttering in my gut, I sideslipped down the launch ramp. Then, with a deep breath, I let my skis run. For a few magical moments I whizzed through the blue-ice slot canyon, at its narrowest less than 3 metres (10 feet) wide. I inhaled the cool winter air as I tried to soak in my millennium-old surroundings, fully immersed in a deep, mysterious pocket of the world. Like rings on a tree, the striated layers of the glacier walls concealed century upon century of natural history, preserved and concealed from any human interference.

Much quicker than I would have liked, I emerged on the far side to join those who had passed before me and were clustered on a snowy slope surrounded by gaping crevasses only a

Icefall Lodge guest Hanna watches as Icefall Lodge owner and mountain guide Larry Dolecki manages the rope before exploring an ice canyon cleaved into a glacier.

few metres away in any direction. Bursting with excitement, we waited to savour the expressions of those yet to come through.

Jubilant, we skied 1400 more metres (4,600 feet) of untracked fresh powder down the glacier, over rolls and through sparsely treed glades for ninety glorious minutes, periodically regrouping, hooting and laughing all the way to valley bottom. All the while, more fresh powder continued falling from opaque clouds.

Skiers and a snowboarder (centre), weave fresh powder turns through seracs on Tempest Glacier, near Icefall Lodge.

While we would have to climb 900 metres (2,950 feet) up a treed valley to reach the lodge – two and half hours for the stronger skiers, an hour longer for a few of us, making my day more than ten hours long – no one complained. Beaming with exhilaration we feasted on dinner and chatted excitedly over the last of our week's wine stash, reliving our day.

Through the course of the winter, Dolecki's 2150-metre (7,100-foot) Tempest Glacier tour was a big hit with subsequent guests, but our group was the very first ever to ski through the ice canyon – my own passage into a mountain adventure of exquisitely possible proportions.

Best seasons: Icefall Lodge is open to guests both summer and winter, which is a very good thing because the massive glaciated terrain that serves up long, interesting and thoroughly enjoyable skiing in the winter also delivers some outstanding mountaineering opportunities in summer. And with two smaller satellite huts, hikers with no mountaineering experience at all can sign up for the adventure of a lifetime, a six-day European-style high alpine traverse: www.icefall.ca.

Trailhead: In winter, Icefall Lodge is accessed by helicopter only, from Golden, BC. Summer access is by helicopter or by a hike which involves a two-hour drive from Golden, much of it on a gravel forestry road. Topo map *Rostrum Peak 82 N/14*.

Families seeking a more luxurious lodge in a true wilderness setting should check out Nipika Lodge, accessed by driving south on Highway 93 South and turning onto Settlers Road, just beyond the boundary of Kootenay National Park's southeast corner. Guided activities include hiking, mountain biking, canoeing and whitewater rafting in summer, plus options for numerous self-guided activities. In winter, Nipika offers a wide range of guided and independent activities, including cross-country skiing, snowshoeing, ice-skating and tobogganing. Visit www.nipika.com.

In winter, the terrain at Icefall Lodge is not suitable for skiers who are not comfortable skiing black diamond runs at a lift-serviced ski resort. In summer, anyone who is keen to spend several hours a day hiking uphill will be rewarded by spectacular views of giant glaciated peaks, tumbling waterfalls, and meadows blanketed with multi-coloured wildflowers. Nestled right at treeline at 1900 metres (6,234 feet), Icefall Lodge is a backcountry skier's dream come true. Big glacier tours, steep and deep powder runs though old-growth cedar forests, and a steady, generous snowfall means fresh tracks day after day. While self-guided weeks are available, the sheer expanse of the terrain means hiring a guide will translate into more vertical skied for every metre of uphill travelling. In summer, hiking options will keep you busy for days, with plenty of vertical to help you earn your dinner, provided by a professional backcountry cook! For the full meal deal, sign up for the guided six-day alpine traverse and experience glacier travel without any exposed technical climbing. Shorter options are also available. See www.icefall.ca.

In winter, base yourself at the lodge and go for the big vertical with the 2200-metre (7,218-foot) Tempest Glacier traverse. Later in the ski season, when the days are longer, or in summer, bag one of the Canadian Rockies 11,000ers, Lyell 5 (Christian Peak), 3390 metres (11,122 feet), or set up a high camp and try and knock off the full Lyells Traverse. For route info, check out *The 11,000ers of the Canadian Rockies*, by Bill Corbett.

Hire a guide: To hire a guide for this and other adventures, go to www.icefall.ca.

12

Glaciologists Probe Icefield Depths To Gauge Mass – and Melting

Walking across the water-polished rocks of a glacial moraine carrying a laptop-sized padded case in one hand and a blue plastic box resembling a textbook in the other, Dr. Mike Demuth, head of the Geological Survey of Canada's glaciology section, looked very much the picture of a man heading off to work.

Which was exactly what he was doing one morning in June 2010 when a helicopter dropped him near a small lake below the toe of Castleguard Glacier, a location that would have taken two days to access on foot.

Stopping at a "ground control point" previously identified from aerial photos, he connected a saucer-shaped antenna to a GPS receiver and programmed it to triangulate its position. Later, the data – accurate to within 10 centimetres (4 inches) – will be used in conjunction with satellite imagery and historical photos to create 3D digital terrain models, employing a technique called photogrammetry, of the Columbia Icefield, for each decade from the 1940s to the present.

This work is one part of how glaciologists from the GSC, with support from the Canadian Space Agency and Parks Canada, are using technology to conduct a complete analysis of the volume of ice contained in the 223-square-kilometre (86-square-mile) Columbia Icefield.

As a hydrological apex, from where water flows to three oceans – Atlantic, Pacific and Arctic – the Columbia Icefield is a valuable reservoir of freshwater feeding three of Canada's major river systems, including the North Saskatchewan. And, like glaciers and icefields the world over, the Canadian Rockies glaciers are shrinking.

"Some three million people live in the North and South Saskatchewan river basins," said Bob Sandford, Canadian chair of the United Nations Water for Life initiative. "From Mike Demuth's research so far, the ice volume wastage estimated for these two basins, expressed as an annual average, is equivalent to the amount of water use of approximately one and a half million people."

While much is known about the relatively accessible Saskatchewan and Athabasca glaciers, the latter of which is seen by two million tourists annually, little is known about the icefield that feeds these and other glaciers.

In April 2010, Demuth and three colleagues skied up the Saskatchewan Glacier to a flat area on the Columbia Icefield

Glaciologists

LOCALS' LORE: *In the summer of 1942, during the Second World War, a road was built from the Icefields Parkway to the toe of the Saskatchewan Glacier so that US troops could access the glacier for training exercises. While it was possible then to drive heavy military vehicles on the actual ice, glacial recession has now rendered that impossible. When the military departed their camp, they left behind a semi-permanent building, which collapsed the following winter. In 1943, the Canadian Army used salvaged materials to build a smaller hut to serve as a training base for the regiment called the Lovat Scouts. The hut was later turned over to the Alpine Club of Canada, providing access to the Saskatchewan Glacier. By the 1960s, however, few people were bothering to hike the 5 kilometres (3 miles) necessary to reach the hut, and it had fallen into disrepair and been undercut by the river. Eventually it was torn down and removed by Parks Canada.*

at the base of Mount Snow Dome. There, Sasha Chichagov, a remote-sensing specialist with Natural Resources Canada, John Sekerka, an NRCan technician and popular camp cook, glaciology technician Steve Bertollo and Demuth rendezvoused with the helicopter that delivered the camping gear, food and scientific equipment they would need to live on the glacier at 2920 metres (9,580 feet) for three weeks.

After carefully probing for crevasses, they established their camp, which included small individual sleeping tents, a communal kitchen tent and outhouse facilities that would be flown out at the end of their stay. They would even be maintaining a helicopter landing pad, in case of emergency. Two volunteers, environmental science student Selena Cordeau and University of Calgary master's candidate Jocelyn Hirose, skied up to join them. For two weeks the team enjoyed great weather and stellar views of surrounding peaks, including the Rockies' second-highest, Mount Columbia, at 3747 metres (12,293 feet), as they carried out measurements to accurately determine the depth of the icefield.

Dragging ground penetrating radar equipment on sleds, the crew recorded radio waves transmitted from the surface through the glacier and reflected back from its internal layers and the glacier bed. Assessing the amount of water stored in glaciers depends on being able to measure their mass, not just their area, and this measurement is hard to do because the composition of the ground the glacier sits on is unknown.

"Knowing something about the thickness of the ice and the info we gain from photogrammetry will help us model what the icefield's fate will be in the future," Demuth said. "How will that impact river flows, public safety, ecosystem integrity, even visitor experience, including the Brewster snowcoach glacier tours?"

Past estimates that the icefield is 350 metres (1,148 feet) thick appear to be exaggerated, as the new data – not yet fully analyzed – suggests the thickness is closer to 150 to 200 metres (492 to 656 feet).

Glaciologists must possess the same safe glacier travel skills as these mountaineers ascending the headwall where the Athabasca Glacier begins to descend from the Columbia Icefield.

In addition to using ground-penetrating radar to map the glacier bed, the researchers are employing airborne LiDAR, a laser-based optical sensing technology similar to radar but much more sensitive. Rich data is collected when laser energy beamed from the aircraft interacts with surface features on the glacier and, upon scattering, returns back to a detector.

"The combination of LiDAR and ground-penetrating radar should yield the first truly accurate measurements of the form and thickness of the Columbia Icefield and how much ice it contains, from which the water equivalent of that ice can be derived," Sandford said. "From these calculations it will then be possible to estimate with a fair degree of predictive accuracy how long individual glaciers and even the Columbia Icefield itself may last under a number of projected climate change scenarios."

That information, Sandford said, should be used to guide policy-makers as water resources in Western Canada decrease as a result of changing weather patterns.

Glaciologist Mike Demuth assembles a GPS receiver and its antenna as part of a research project to map and measure the volume of ice contained in the Columbia Icefield.

During their research expedition, Demuth and his team recorded evidence of just those changes.

When stormy weather kept them tent-bound for much of their third week, the research was paused as they were forced to dig out their tents every six hours. To escape boredom, they eventually skied up Snow Dome in a whiteout to drill a shallow ice core to look at melt layers.

"Interestingly, there was lots of melting in the middle of this last winter at 11,000 feet [3353 metres]," Demuth said. "We're not talking just a little glaze-crust sun layer, but massive ice layer development, really strong melting, which is unusual at that elevation in the middle of winter."

A Calgary native and keen mountaineer currently based in Ottawa, Ontario, Canada's capital, Demuth helps oversee monitoring of a network of Western Canada's glaciers and he'd been aware of successive weeks of sunny, above-freezing weather in the

Rockies through much of February and March. Demuth hopes to return with a different instrument to drill a smaller-diameter, much deeper hole to gain a longer perspective on the melting.

"Then we can ask, is this melting we saw last winter unusual?" Demuth said. "Are mid-winter melt events becoming more frequent?"

Such information is valuable from many standpoints, including compiling "state of the park" reports every five years, explained Bill Fisher, Parks Canada's director general for Western and Northern Canada.

"We [Parks] have an obligation to monitor a whole variety of things, not just glaciers," Fisher said. "It's important for us to work with the experts and to support them, help with things like logistics."

Parks can also highlight the uniqueness of having a triple watershed within a single national park, to share the message of what's happening to glaciers around the world by incorporating the new scientific information into the upgrading of the Columbia Icefield Visitors' Centre.

"There are few spots in the world where this many people can get close enough to see a glacier," Fisher said. "With this research, we can tell a more compelling story in real time. We can tell a global story, and we can tell it right here. If we're going to talk about the glacier story, this is the best place in North America to do that. People from everywhere come here."

Best seasons: To be sure, the vast majority of people who visit the Columbia Icefield do so from June to September. And many of those visitors can attest that the area is not always the most hospitable environment, even at the peak of summer! Regardless of the conditions of the moment, though, whether it's beaming sunshine and a clear, robin's-egg-blue sky or screeching winds and nasty –40° temperatures (Celsius and Fahrenheit meet at –40°), the Columbia Icefield and its accessible Saskatchewan and Athabasca glaciers are always fascinating and very special places to see. It is important to note, however, that in winter the Icefields Parkway is a very quiet, lonely road traversing high, windswept passes with no services between Lake Louise and Jasper, and should not be attempted without proper winter tires and survival gear should you become stuck overnight in a severe – and entirely possible – storm.

Trailhead: The Parker Ridge trailhead, located 41 kilometres (25.5 miles) north of Saskatchewan River Crossing, or the Saskatchewan Glacier Basin trailhead, 34 kilometres (21 miles) north of Saskatchewan River Crossing, both offer excellent starting points for day hikes leading to glaciers fed by the Columbia Icefield. Always pack a warm layer, rain jacket, toque and gloves; you can be soaking up the sunshine in short sleeves one day and catching snowflakes on your tongue the next, any month of the year! Topo map *Columbia Icefield 83 C/3.*

Parker Ridge, 2.4 kilometres (1.5 miles), 280 metres (919 feet) elevation gain, high point 2280 metres (7,480 feet).

This well-graded trail gently switchbacks up the slopes of Parker Ridge, topping out on a saddle from where you'll be rewarded with a spectacular climber's eye view overlooking the 12-kilometre (7.5-mile) tongue of the Saskatchewan Glacier, which descends from the massive Columbia Icefield. Be sure to check with Parks Canada at 780.852.6176 to make sure the trail is open if you're planning your hike before mid-July.

Saskatchewan Glacier Basin, 6 kilometres (3.7 miles), elevation gain 155 metres (500 feet).

While this hike serves up much less vertical than the Parker Ridge route, its destination at the toe of the Saskatchewan Glacier in a remote and entirely natural wilderness setting is well worth the visit. But don't even think about walking onto glacial ice without a guide, a rope and crevasse rescue experience.

Castleguard Meadows backpack, 35 kilometres (22 miles), 610 metres (2,000 feet) elevation gain, high point 2135 metres (7,000 feet). Topo maps *Columbia Icefield, 83 C/3, Cline River 83 C/2.*

There are two approach routes for reaching the extremely remote and fascinating Castleguard Meadows. One is to follow the hiking trail to the toe of the Saskatchewan Glacier, then hike another 5 kilometres (3 miles) up the glacier, but only if you are experienced and well equipped to do so.

If you enjoy real – and rough – wilderness travel without the skills required to walk on a glacier, follow the Icefields Parkway 26 kilometres (16 miles) north of Saskatchewan River Crossing to the junction with the Alexandra River fire road. Watch for a pullout at a viewpoint on the west side of the road, overlooking a narrow canyon. While the first 20 kilometres of the journey follows a roadbed, after 11.5 kilometres (7 miles) numerous braided river channels have washed out the road, making travel more difficult. Spend the night at the campsite at 21.5 kilometres (13.4 miles), then continue on a rocky, rooty hiking trail to the Castleguard Meadows campsite and explore the spectacular treeline environment. See *The Canadian Rockies Trail Guide*, by Brian Patton and Bart Robinson.

Bust a Lung! Mount Columbia, 3747 metres (12,293 feet), East Face II; South Ridge II. Topo map *Columbia Icefield 83 C/3*.

Most parties approach by the shorter, albeit more exposed Athabasca Glacier, but some take the longer Saskatchewan Glacier route, which does not involve crossing under a sérac field. For a full route description, check out *The 11,000ers of the Canadian Rockies*, by Bill Corbett.

Hire a guide: If you don't have the requisite skills and experience, hire a guide to take you on any of these adventures or to organize a custom trip: www.acmg.ca, www.yamnuska.com or www.internationalguidebureau.com.

Icefield Adventure Delivers Chilling Lessons

I t was really cold at the Columbia Icefield parking lot. I knew that, even before I got out of my car – which I didn't do until after I'd put on my ski boots and before turning off the engine and with it the vehicle's interior heater. Cast out into the frigid air, I reluctantly joined my tripmates who were industriously stuffing tent sections, food items and canisters of camp stove fuel into their backpacks, intermittently jumping around and windmilling their arms trying to stay warm, despite being dressed in down jackets and balaclavas.

Yup, it was the last weekend in March, and the temperature at the Athabasca Glacier upper parking lot was definitely below –20°C (-4°F).

No worries, I thought. It's only 8 a.m. and the sky is clear. We just have to wait for the sun to climb above the top of Mount Andromeda and it'll warm us as we ski up the Athabasca Glacier to gain the Columbia Icefield.

I'd wanted to experience such a trip for years – camping overnight on the Columbia Icefield and living for a few days completely immersed in the world of glacier, snow and high alpine wilderness.

After countless ski-touring days and nights in alpine huts in the Canadian Rockies and Selkirk Mountains, plus several nights winter camping below treeline in Jasper and Rogers Pass in BC's Glacier National Park, I'd also camped on des Poilus Glacier while travelling the Bow–Yoho traverse. I was confident I could manage a few nights on the Columbia Icefield. As soon as Alpine Club of Canada volunteer trip leaders Brian Merry and Dominic Fredette posted a five-night Columbia Icefield trip, I signed up.

Hoisting my 50-plus-pound pack onto my 130-pound, five-foot-four-inch body, my most immediate concern shifted to wondering how I was going to manage the weight skinning uphill for a seven-hour day. But then all nine of us, including my friend Gail Crowe-Swords, the only other woman on the trip, knew big, heavy packs were just part of the adventure, which would hopefully include ski ascents of the North and South Twin, Mount Kitchener, Snow Dome and maybe even Stutfield Peak.

LOCALS' LORE: *The first non-Aboriginal people – quite likely the first humans ever – to witness the sight of the immense Columbia Icefield were the British explorers J. Norman Collie and Herman Woolley, when they became the first to climb to Mount Athabasca's 3491-metre (11,453-foot) summit in 1898. While modern mountaineers drive to the mountain's base in a matter of hours from Canmore, Banff, Jasper or even Calgary or Edmonton, or in mere minutes from several nearby campgrounds or HI-Hilda Creek Wilderness Hostel, Collie and Woolley's approach involved an 18-day, 240-kilometre (149-mile) expedition by horseback from Laggan – now Lake Louise. Theirs was one of the most significant moments in the history of mountaineering in Canada, of which Collie wrote:*
"The view that lay before us in the evening light was one that does not often fall to the lot of modern mountaineers. A new world was spread at our feet; to the westward stretched a vast icefield probably never before seen by human eye, and surrounded by entirely unknown, unnamed and unclimbed peaks."

Ski mountaineers skin up slowly under the weight of heavy packs carrying everything they'll need for five nights of camping on the Columbia Icefield.

As we made our way to the glacier's north flank, the sun finally reached us but still it offered little warmth. Despite my sturdy Gore-Tex jacket on top of several other layers, plus a balaclava, a quick stop for a drink and snack rendered my fingers painfully frozen inside my big insulated mitts, even with a pair of polypro liners inside. Well accustomed to my fast-to-freeze fingers, I eagerly pressed on, in the knowledge that moving, especially uphill, would soon thaw them out.

We continued up the glacier, skiing steadily through the field of ice boulders that had crashed down from the glimmering blue séracs on the steep slopes above on our right. To our left, a cascading icefall resembled a sea of angry, roiling waves with smooth-polished valleys and peaks of ice glinting in the sun. After three hours we stopped for lunch at the base of the headwall that would lead to the névé above.

Despite the sun, I was cold. I ate heartily, knowing my body could generate more heat if I was well fed. But I also knew, as

I shivered in my down jacket, that I was colder than I should have been. Generally, I avoid ski touring in temperatures below –20°C (–4°F), since the cold aggravates my asthma, with which I have little or no trouble in warmer temperatures. But then, I knew I'd be fine as soon as we started moving again, especially since we'd have to ski up the steep headwall immediately after the break. Uphill travel always generates more body heat.

But the little voice in my head was saying something else: "I should not be attempting to camp in weather this cold." That thought, however, was followed by "I have to at least try." Apart from the cold, I was doing fine. By far the smallest person in the group, I was keeping up and had easily passed one of the men, who wasn't moving as steadily as I was. I had accepted the weight of my pack, and the reality that this would simply be a long, slow, heavy, challenging day. I was at peace with thoughts of the most basic pleasures – hot soup and dehydrated dinner, tea and the –40°-rated sleeping bag I'd borrowed.

Finally, by 3:30 p.m. the sun's brilliant rays began to warm us. For the first time all day, I opened my outer jacket to let out some body heat and stashed my inner glove liners inside a pocket as we skinned up the gently inclining yet seemingly endless snow slope. Just before 5 p.m. we stopped to set up camp, carefully probing the area for crevasses before pitching our tents. For the next two hours the sun was a welcome friend as we busied ourselves stomping out platforms in the snow, erecting our tents and melting snow for water for dinner. Life was good.

The blue sky was streaked with pure white contrails from jets. To our west and south, the horizon was fenced with a panorama of jagged, rocky summits. Poking above their gleaming white neighbours were 3507-metre (11,506-foot) Mount Bryce and farther south the dramatic summit pyramid of 3612-metre (11,850-foot) Mount Forbes.

My joy was not to last. With sunset the temperature dropped quickly and my shivering returned. Hurrying to exchange my ski boots for my insulated booties, I hunkered inside the tent

Author Lynn Martel enjoys the view and the last warm rays of sun before nightfall at 3048 metres (10,000 feet) on the Columbia Icefield.

I was sharing with Gail and changed into dry socks. The task was exhausting and laborious, my breathing strained and rapid. I puffed repeatedly on my bronchial inhaler. Finally I crawled into my sleeping bag while Gail and the others chatted outside and casually commented on the sudden drop in temperature. Brian's thermometer registered –24°C (–11°F), but the clear evening was likely to grow colder.

Cocooned in three pairs of pants and five layers on my torso topped by my down jacket, I managed to achieve a state of tolerable warmth inside my sleeping bag, my head wrapped in a toque, down hood and sleeping bag hood. Still, occasional shivers penetrated deep inside my core.

I barely slept.

Come morning, I had but one thought: home. Off this glacier. Cloud cover had created whiteout conditions, and while the temperature had risen to –18°C (0°F) there was unlikely to be any sun that day to provide any further warmth. The previous day's asthma attacks and efforts to maintain warmth had left me quite drained.

As I lay in my bag, comfortable on two sleeping pads, condensation from the nylon tent ceiling sprinkled on my face. I laughed at myself for not harbouring any doubts about what I needed to do.

I fully accept that things won't always be fun in the mountains. I've been buried up to my neck in an avalanche. I've seen a comrade be dug up blue – and miraculously alive – after being buried half an hour. I've been cold more times than I can count, my hands numb many more times than I care to recall. I've been a lot more sore from carrying a heavy pack – and way more scared and tired – than I ever wanted to be.

As a long-time Bow Valley resident and avid mountain adventurer, I've long been aware of the far above average expectations the local community places on itself. No wonder. Canmore is home to some of the most daring and prolific adventurers in the world and to a raft of Olympic athletes, including a few medal winners. Our local bar is a high one. As another wave of light shivers brushed across my torso and penetrated my core, I peacefully admitted I was not one of them, and that was just fine by me.

To their credit, Dominic and Brian never doubted or second-guessed my resolute decision that I needed to get down off the icefield. Dominic valiantly volunteered to shorten his trip and accompany me for safety.

"I've got a family, and I've got a couple more trips planned up here this year," Dominic said. "And there's soccer on – Chelsea's playing!"

With Gail manning our stove I filled my belly with instant oatmeal and a two-cup mug of steaming tea, then set about the task of refilling my pack. By 11:30 a.m. Dominic and I set out across the nearly flat ocean of snow. The world was silent and calm, visibility limited to the séracs on the lower slopes of Snow Dome that appeared like ominous sculptures in the silhouetted light as we slowly glided past. At the top of the headwall ramp we stopped for a minute to rest our legs before making the steepest downhill turns of the day under our big heavy packs. A few minutes later we had descended the slope, both pleased to have accomplished the run without falling.

As we were approaching the parking lot, just before 2 p.m., Dominic commented on our having camped above 3048 metres (10,000 feet). Later I gave that fact some thought. I had been shivering up there, at times slightly nauseous, short of breath, with headaches (which I attributed to not drinking enough water during the day), had slept little and felt utterly fatigued – all symptoms of altitude sickness. Although I had once camped as high as 4250 metres (13,944 feet) in Peru, where I'd hiked up to 4760 metres (15,617 feet), I was well acclimatized when I did, having lived above 3048 metres for several weeks. And though I'd climbed above 3000 metres in the Rockies many times, and slept in two huts above 2900 metres (9,514 feet), I'd never attempted such a thing in temperatures below -20°.

Had I experienced some altitude sickness? I don't know. But I do know I'd like to go back – in July!

AUTHOR'S NOTE: *I was actually offered a chance to return to the Columbia Icefield for a multi-day camping and peak-bagging adventure in July that year, but I turned the trip down. I simply wasn't ready to spend a week on snow, particularly since summer in the Canadian Rockies is sooo fleeting! I headed to the Bugaboos in BC's Purcell Mountains for a few days of hot, sunny mountaineering adventures instead. Summer camping on the Icefield, however, is still on my bucket list ...*

Best seasons: Unless you're an experienced climber or ski mountaineer, the best time to visit the Columbia Icefield area is definitely in summer. But if you don't mind camping in -30°C (-22°F) or suffering through the inevitable wind-whipped whiteouts while waiting patiently for a blue-sky summit day, then the Columbia Icefield is one of the most easily accessed multi-day glaciated mountaineering destination in North America. The Icefield Centre, however, is only open from May 1 thru October 15: www.pc.gc.ca.

Trailhead: Athabasca Glacier and the Columbia Icefield are located along the Icefields Parkway, 126 kilometres (78 miles) north of the Trans-Canada Highway interchange, or 104 kilometres (65 miles) south of Jasper. Stay at one of several campsites, www.pc.gc.ca, or at the Glacier View Inn, www.explorerockies.com.

Topo map *Columbia Icefield 83 C/3, Sunwapta Peak 83 C/6.*

Family Friendly

As one of the most visited sites in the entire Canadian Rockies – for excellent reasons – the Columbia Icefield's Athabasca Glacier tour is a family-friendly activity that should not be missed. Riding aboard a specially designed Brewster Ice Explorer, your experienced step-on guide will share a mountain's worth of information during the ride out onto the ice. Make sure to wear flat, rubber-soled shoes so you can step out onto the actual ice. NEVER VENTURE – NOT EVEN A SHORT DISTANCE – ONTO A GLACIER WITHOUT A GUIDE. Visit www.explorerockies.com.

Wheelchair access: One-quarter of Brewster's Ice Explorer fleet vehicles are wheelchair accessible. The regular shuttle vans that deliver guests to the Explorer vehicles are not chair-accessible, however, so it is necessary to book a spot in a specially equipped van. Visit www.explorerockies.com.

Sweat a Little

Rather than riding onto the glacier, sign up for a guided walk with a professional – and knowledgeable – guide. Take the three-hour Ice Cubed tour or try the longer Icewalk Deluxe Tours, which run from three to six hours. They'll even equip you with small crampons to fit over your own hiking boots, or you can use a pair of theirs. Don't forget to bring your camera! Visit http://icewalks.com for details.

Or hike up to Wilcox Pass, 4 kilometres (2.5 miles), 335 metres (1,100 feet) elevation gain, high point 2375 metres (7,800 feet).

While walking on the glacier is not to be missed, the hike up Wilcox Pass provides a raven's-eye view of that glacier and the peaks surrounding it. As a bonus, by mid-July the high alpine meadows will be splattered with a candy-store display's worth of colourful wildflowers. You'll find the trailhead at Wilcox Creek Campground on the east side of the highway, 2.8 kilometres (1.7 miles) south of the Icefield Centre.

Sunwapta Peak, easy scramble, 7 to 12 hours, 1735 metres (5,692 feet) elevation gain, high point 3315 metres (10,876 feet).

Start at the Stanley Falls hiking trail sign, 15.6 kilometres (9.7 miles) north of the Icefield Centre. Don't follow the trail south to Stanley Falls, but rather walk north for a few minutes to a stream with a gravel berm. Hike up the left side of the drainage, then angle to your right toward the ridge and keep on trudging all the way to the summit. Pack a big lunch and lots of water! For a full route description, check out *Scrambles in the Canadian Rockies*, by Alan Kane.

Mount Athabasca, North Glacier II, 1450 metre (4,757 feet) elevation gain, high point 3491 metres (11,453 feet).

With its proximity and impressive visibility from the road, Athabasca is understandably the most popular alpine climb in the Columbia Icefield area. It is not the only one, however, so if you've got the skills, you'll find full route details for mounts Andromeda, North Twin, Twins Tower, West Twin, Stutfield, Kitchener and Snow Dome, as well as the Rockies' second-highest, the 3747-metre (12,293-foot) Mount Columbia, in *The 11,000ers of the Canadian Rockies*, by Bill Corbett.

Ice climbing: The Weeping Wall, located 28.6 kilometres (17.8 miles) north of Saskatchewan River Crossing, is undoubtedly Canada's best-known ice-climbing venue. From November to May the 600-metre-high (1,969-foot) cliffs are home to dozens of waterfalls created by melting snow and seeps initiating higher up on the west-facing slopes of 3270-metre (10,728-foot) Cirrus Mountain. Routes range from 40 to 300 metres (131 to 984 feet) in length, and WI3 to WI6 in difficulty, plus numerous mixed lines.

 See *Waterfall Ice: Climbs in the Canadian Rockies*, by Joe Josephson. Open throughout the winter and complete with fully equipped kitchen facilities, heated dorm rooms and a wood-burning sauna building, HI-Rampart Creek Wilderness Hostel provides an excellent base camp: www.hihostels.ca.

Hire a guide: If you don't have the requisite skills and experience, or you want to improve the skills you do have, hire a guide to take you on any of these adventures or to organize a custom trip: www.acmg.ca, www.yamnuska.com or www.internationalguidebureau.com.

Fun and Games until Your Shoes Get Wet

I can tell before I open my eyes that moisture is falling from the sky – the fine drizzly stuff that's not rain but not quite snow. Crisp air glides through the open window a metre from my face, and just as I pull my sleeping bag around my head a cheery voice offers me some tea.

Dave has been up for a while already, the woodstove is warming the single room of the Alpine Club of Canada's Sydney Vallance (Fryatt) Hut and now I'm being offered tea in bed. This is the life.

My buddy Andrea Pintaric is also up and after a few sips I join her and Dave for a breakfast of instant oatmeal, the prepackaged kind we'd never eat at home but which somehow always tastes just fine in the mountains. For his first time in a hut, his first time even in the mountains, Dave, a Manitoba Hydro manager from Winnipeg who runs marathons, is a wonderful host.

Outside, thick grey clouds swarm around the peaks and upper slopes spackled in snow. Suddenly the light dims as a moving mass of fog engulfs the upper valley. This calls for a game of cribbage.

Between squalls, Andrea, Dave and I hike up the ridge that tops the north flank of the headwall, following a tight, steep trail through alders heavy with frost and water that quickly soaks our pants. As we step carefully from wet rock to slick dirt I can't help but wonder how difficult it had to have been for Xin and Ke, the young Chinese couple now warm and dry by the woodstove, to negotiate yesterday after losing their way hiking to the hut.

Andrea and I had met them the day before, around 5:45 p.m. at Headwall Campground, below the notoriously steep final climb to the cabin. Both of them were dressed in jeans and our eyes were drawn immediately to Ke's feet. She had hiked more than 24 kilometres (15 miles) of damp, root-strewn, rocky trails in a pair of red cotton canvas high-top sneakers. They were unloading crackers, cheese and Spam from a big pack, with Ke's daypack on the ground nearby. They had no stove and told us they had been cold in their leaky tent and summer-weight sleeping bags the previous night.

We suggested – rather insistently – that they stay at the hut, less than a kilometre farther on. Shortly before, we had passed Tim, the hut custodian, and his friend Hamish on their way down the trail. They were hiking out two days early, having risen at 3 a.m. for three consecutive mornings to climb Mount Fryatt, only to find it covered in fresh snow and verglas. They assured us the hut would be nearly empty.

Xin asked how to get there and I replied, pointing in the direction, "Follow the trail."

Andrea and I reached the hut half an hour later, made Dave's acquaintance and quickly headed back down, thinking Ke might need a little help up the steep, slippery section. We reached the campsite without seeing them. Maybe they'd hiked back down the valley, we shrugged. On the way back up both of us wondered if we heard voices, but no one answered our calls.

Shortly after 9 p.m., we heard a shout from outside. It was Ke and Xin. Quickly we ushered them in through the vestibule. Ke was trembling, partly from the cold and partly the result of

Max Schoffel rides his mountain bike on the approach to Fryatt Valley.

Alex Wright (left) and Max Schoffel admire the view of Tonquin Valley's Ramparts far in the distance (slightly right of centre) from a high col in Upper Fryatt Valley.

LOCALS' LORE: *Mount Fryatt was named in 1920 by the Boundary Commission, after Charles Fryatt, captain of the merchant ship* Brussels, *which was captured by German U-boats during the First World War. After his captors accused him of trying to ram a submarine, Fryatt was summarily shot. Many peaks throughout the Canadian Rockies have names connected to First and Second World War battles and heroes. Sydney Vallance (Fryatt) Hut is named for Sydney R. Vallance, QC, who served as Alpine Club of Canada president from 1947 to 1950. He died in 1979.*

being terrified at the thought of spending another night outside, this time lost. They had missed the trail and bushwhacked up the seriously steep headwall far to the right, somehow stumbling upon the upper ridge trail, which they followed down to the hut.

I was so relieved, but at the same time wondered whether Andrea and I, by suggesting they stay at the hut in the first place, might have almost caused an epic.

"We were so lucky to find this place," Xin said.

Ke had never camped or hiked before. Xin was strong and robust. He'd been living in Ontario for four years, working on his Ph.D. in food sciences at the University of Guelph. Ke was studying English as a second language in Vancouver. They had hitchhiked from Jasper to Athabasca Falls and walked to the first campsite from there, more than 14 kilometres (8.7 miles). They carried a 1978 second edition of Patton and Robinson's *The Canadian Rockies Trail Guide*. They devoured all the warm food offered them and I wished I had brought extra, especially soup.

On the ridge, the clouds separate slightly as rock cairns come into sight. Below, Fryatt Lake is a bold burst of turquoise colour in a world of grey and green rock and trees. Everything above treeline is festively covered in fresh snow. We hike across lumpy meadows of heather to a jewel-toned tarn ringed with lichen-speckled boulders. We continue down to another, larger lake, twenty minutes above the hut, and spot Xin and Ke on the opposite bank. I'm glad to see them out enjoying the splendour of glacier-fed lakes and high alpine flowers, but wonder if they notice the approaching storm clouds.

We reach the hut just ahead of the squall and are soon joined by Greg and Erica from Seattle, who are camping in the lower valley. We offer them tea, and then do the same for Dan from Boston, who's playing hooky from a conference in computational biology in Edmonton, a five-hour drive from the trailhead. Soon afterward, Noel from Stony Plain, Alberta, arrives for the night. Xin and Ke burst through the door, wet again, and place their soggy shoes by the fire.

Funny, I think, how August snow squalls are so much more tolerable when you're socializing in a woodstove-heated hut.

After the campers leave, I ask Ke what she thinks of backpacking.

She hesitates, shaking her head slightly. "It's unforgettable, for sure."

Suddenly there's a racket on the roof. It's hailing and the sun is shining. Dave and Noel, who coincidentally works for TransAlta, are talking shop.

The great thing about visiting a hut for a few days is the way I feel transported to an entirely different world and how each hut has its own personality and charms. And I appreciate how Fryatt Hut's plentiful windows provide such a comfortable theatre for viewing the alpenglow.

The crib game resumes. Dave is an intense, positively possessed player. I decide card playing isn't really fun until the players' personalities become part of the game.

We wake up to more snow and Dave, Andrea and I hike out, giving Xin and Ke a three-and-a-half-hour head start. Dave recovers his bike at the halfway campsite and rides off ahead of us. When Andrea and I reach the parking lot after a six-and-a-half-hour hike we find a note on the windshield. Forty-five minutes earlier, Ke and Xin had changed into dry clothes and Dave had given them a lift to Jasper so they could rent a car and begin their next adventure.

Best seasons: In summertime, the Upper Fryatt Valley is a remote and delightful destination for hikers and mountaineers alike, while several valley bottom trails offer wonderful shorter destinations for day hikers and mountain bikers. In winter, the area offers numerous options for cross-country skiers, snowshoers and experienced backcountry skiers. To book your spot at Sydney Vallance (Fryatt) Hut, visit www.alpineclubofcanada.ca.

Trailhead: Follow the Icefields Parkway to Athabasca Falls, 31 kilometres (19.3 miles) south of Jasper, and turn west onto Highway 93A. Follow 93A for 1.2 kilometres (0.75 miles) to the Geraldine Lake fire road, then follow this well-graded fire road for 2.1 kilometres (1.3 miles) to the Fryatt Valley trailhead. For Geraldine Lakes, drive 5.5 kilometres (3.4 miles) to the parking lot at the end of the road. Topo maps *Athabasca Falls 83 C/12, Fortress Lake 83 C/5.*

Lower Geraldine Lake, 1.8 kilometres (1.1 miles), 130 metres (427 feet) elevation gain, high point 1610 metres (5,282 feet).

Tucked between the steep, towering summits of Mount Fryatt and Whirlpool Peak, the first of the four Geraldine Lakes is a pleasant 45-minute stroll along a well-travelled trail.

Second Geraldine Lake, 5 kilometres (3 miles), 410 metres (1,345 feet) elevation gain, high point 1890 metres (6,200 feet).

From the far end of the first lake the trail climbs steeply for 300 metres (984 feet) alongside a 90-metre (295-foot) waterfall that tumbles over successive rock steps to the lake below. Beyond a small tarn the trail climbs steeply alongside another waterfall that is even more spectacular than the first, reaching an exceptionally fine viewpoint that provides a much-appreciated rest stop a few minutes before the second lake.

Fryatt Hut, 22 kilometres (13.7 miles), 820 metres (2,700 feet) elevation gain, high point 2040 metres (6,700 feet).

The first half of the distance is through forest with little scenery, following a relatively flat, broad trail that can be covered on foot or by mountain bike, arriving at Lower Fryatt Campground, located next to Fryatt Creek and the bridge that crosses it. Bikes are not permitted beyond this point. This campground offers an excellent stopover for those not keen on covering the entire distance in one day. From here the trail winds up through forest, then crosses the rushing creek again over a solid bridge. Beyond, the trail traverses a massive rockslide, then skirts around Fryatt Lake before heading steeply up the final headwall to the hut. If you carried a beer all the way up there, you'll have really earned your reward! Be sure to stay at least two nights so you'll have time to explore the amazing quartzite and conglomerate boulder fields above the hut, and even take in the fabulous view to the north from a small, unnamed scrambling peak. To book your spot in the hut, visit www.alpineclubofcanada.ca/facility/fryatt.html.

Mount Fryatt, 3361 metres (11,027 feet), Southwest Face, II, 5.4, or West Ridge, III, 5.6, 5.8 for direct finish.

As one of the most dominant peaks bordering the Icefields Parkway, Mount Fryatt is a tantalizing objective for any mountaineer. The fact that it's one of the Canadian Rockies peaks taller than 3353 metres (11,000 feet) adds icing on the cake.

❄ WINTER FUN

Snowshoeing and cross-country skiing: In winter, cross-country skiers and snowshoers can explore a variety of accessible and groomed – for skiers – trails from Highway 93A, which is plowed for 20 kilometres (12.4 miles) south from Jasper to the

Meeting of the Waters picnic site. To rent equipment, visit www.jasperadventurecentre.com. For ski lessons or guided tours or to experience the unique Maligne Canyon Icewalk, go to www.overlandertrekking.com. For snowshoe tours, visit www.walksntalks.com. For trail maps, stop in to the Parks Canada Information Centre in Jasper and pick up a free Winter Trails brochure.

Whirlpool Campground Loop, 4.5 kilometres (2.8 miles), no elevation gain, high point 1130 metres (3,707 feet).

From the Meeting of the Waters parking lot, ski south for 2.2 kilometres (1.4 miles) to the Whirlpool River bridge, then turn left and circle back through the campsite to the parking lot, skiing parallel to the Whirlpool River.

Moab Lake Trail, 18 kilometres (11 miles) return, 110 metres (361 feet) elevation gain, high point 1130 metres (3,707 feet).

From the Meeting of the Waters parking lot, ski south for 2 kilometres (1.2 miles), then turn right onto the Whirlpool River fire road. Ski 6.5 kilometres (4 miles) to what is the summer parking lot and trailhead. Continue about 500 metres (550 yards) farther until you see the sign for Moab Lake directing you to the right. The lake is just down the hill.

Experienced backcountry skiers can shorten the approach to Fryatt Hut by parking at a pullout on the Icefields Parkway 7.5 kilometres (4.7 miles) south of Athabasca Falls and skiing across the Athabasca River, provided it's solidly frozen. Once across the river you'll intersect the summer trail, which you can follow to the hut. Be sure to save some energy for the headwall! Beyond the hut you'll find plenty of enticing touring terrain, but be aware – this is uncontrolled avalanche terrain.

Hire a guide: If you don't have the requisite skills and experience, or you want to improve the skills you do have, hire a guide to take you on any of these adventures or to organize a custom trip: www.acmg.ca, www.yamnuska.com or www.internationalguidebureau.com.

Backyard Bike Tour
Full of Discovery

"Mark, check out these guys' faces biking up this hill," chuckled Bill with just a hint of apprehension as the van transporting us descended the steep hill from Tangle Falls.

We – five men from California, Colorado, Connecticut and New York – plus me, plus Peter Weiland, our tour guide and support van driver, and Dieter, his father and tour assistant, were relaxing on the four-hour drive from Banff to Jasper, from where the following morning we would begin our own five-day, 300-kilometre (186-mile) Icefields Parkway cycling adventure. And Bill knew that day two of our ride would involve pedalling up the steep north side of the Tangle Falls hill.

As a long-time Bow Valley local and avid mountain adventurer, I wasn't worried about cycling uphill. Unlike the five other guests who'd signed up for the tour, which came complete with hotel stays, restaurant meals and a support van, I'd already cycled from Banff to Jasper sixteen years earlier in two and half days, carrying panniers filled with a sleeping bag for hostel stays, food and extra clothing. And I'd ridden it solo.

And although I hadn't pedalled my bike for more than a grocery store run in my small-town home of Canmore in the past decade, I'd maintained above average fitness through those years with regular and intensive backcountry skiing and mountaineering adventures. With my birthday falling during the cycle trip, this guided adventure – something different for me – had come as a gift I couldn't refuse.

No, my biggest concern was whether spending five days cycling the Icefields Parkway would be too familiar an experience to quench my thirst for outdoor adventure. Granted, this is unquestionably one of the world's most stunning stretches of road, justifiably a coveted destination for millions of visitors annually from all over the globe. But for me it had become routinely familiar as just an approach route to trailheads from which I frequently launched multi-day wilderness trips.

In other words, would I be bored exploring pavement in my own backyard?

Native peoples, including the Stoney Nakoda, are known to have travelled this route for hundreds, if not thousands, of years, although they made no mention of a trail as such. For Europeans, the first recorded use of the route between Laggan – now known around the world as Lake Louise – and the North Saskatchewan River happened in 1858. Travelling on horseback, James Hector and his party followed the Bow River north to Hector Lake, where they set up camp. The next day, they continued to Bow Lake, over Bow Summit and on to Waterfowl Lakes, where they camped for the second night. The following day they rode to the North Saskatchewan River.

It wasn't until the Great Depression that construction began on the Banff–Jasper Highway, in the early 1930s. At the peak of the project, crews totalling 625 men worked their way toward each other, southward from Jasper and northward from Lake Louise. They met at the Big Bend just south of the Columbia Icefield, proud to have completed the 6.5-metre (21-foot) wide, 230-kilometre (143-mile) gravel road. Opened in 1940, the "Wonder Road" helped triple the number of visitors to Banff National Park that first year.

No wonder, really. The views of sparkling turquoise,

glacier-fed lakes, tumbling glaciers and chiselled, rocky peaks that line the road are jaw-dropping in intensity and abundance. The route also offers plentiful wildlife viewing of bighorn sheep, elk, mountain goats, black bears and grizzlies.

After checking in at the Jasper Inn and mounting our tour-supplied hybrid bikes, we took a forty-five-minute test spin around the townsite before dinner. By 9 a.m. the next day, with Peter – a surprisingly calm and relaxed former Eco Challenge competitor – driving, and the spry and fit seventy-year-old Dieter pedalling easily ahead of half the group of mostly forty-somethings, we quickly settled into our own paces.

About an hour outside Jasper, I pulled up to the support van at the parking lot at the base of Edith Cavell Road just behind Dan and Mark. While the others, including the perpetually content Dieter, chose the Peter-chauffeured van ride up the 12-kilometre (7.5-mile) Edith Cavell Road, I was feeling strong and confident and decided to cycle the optional leg with Dan and Mark. We all rendezvoused at the Edith Cavell lookout, where I felt excited watching the American men witness their first glacier up close as chunks of ice crashed into the lake.

But by the time we reached our hotel at Sunwapta Falls, just in time for dinner after an 88-kilometre (55-mile) first day out, I feared I may have overestimated my physical ability, as I arrived wet and chilled to the bone from a frosty mountain drizzle. I was also hungry and tired enough to know I was close to bonking after battling a vicious headwind for the last 20 kilometres (12.4 miles). I was certain that for the rest of my life I wouldn't be able to drive that section of the Parkway without cursing that headwind. I graciously accepted my room key from Peter, then indulged guiltily in the longest shower of my life before devouring a decadent restaurant dinner.

Miraculously, I awoke refreshed, as did the others. Breakfast conversation centered on the steep Tangle Falls climb, and whether we might be so fortunate as to see a bear. For the

Cyclists ride into early morning sunlight after overnight showers have moistened the Icefields Parkway near Sunwapta Falls in Jasper National Park.

first two hours the Parkway was our own traffic-free bike path hemmed by rough-edged rock summits. The previous night's rain clouds slowly lifted to reveal snow-strafed cliffbands high on the mountain slopes. Pedalling quietly along on my immaculately tuned bike, I was mesmerized by creeks gushing through culverts that I could always hear for several minutes before I rolled over them. Spellbound, I watched an osprey sitting by the riverbank mere metres from me, its brown tail feathers glinting in the sunlight. Halfway up the big Tangle Falls hill, Peter had parked the van in a pullout and set out patio chairs and a buffet table, from which we hungry cyclists loaded our plates with crispy salad and freshly barbecued chicken. Pedalling toward the Columbia Icefield, mounts Athabasca and Andromeda grew larger and larger down the road ahead, like the Grinch's heart, looming in the landscape many times bigger from our saddles than they had ever appeared when viewed from a car.

By the time we reached our hotel at the Columbia Icefield Centre, one of the great overnight destinations in the Rockies, overlooking the massive Athabasca Glacier, three of the men had indeed seen a bear when they had stopped to fix a flat tire. The rest of us, pedalling ahead of them, had missed it. With much of the afternoon still ahead, Peter drove us all down the road to Parker Ridge for a short hike. Looking down on the Saskatchewan Glacier from the ridgetop, I realized that in two decades of Rockies adventures I had never hiked that trail before.

Unlike our southern guests, I was not surprised by fresh snow on the ground in mid-August – after all, we were above 2135 metres (7,000 feet). I had even packed my ski mitts. So far on this trip I had learned that staying warm on an Icefields Parkway bike tour is a tricky balancing act between too many layers on the climbs and too few on the descents. Later, Peter told us it was the coldest week he'd ever experienced in nine years of running the Icefields tour – the olive oil had even frozen in the van overnight. Indeed, the summer had been a lot like summer used to be in the Rockies: a few warm sunny days followed by a couple of really cool rainy ones, unlike more recent summers, which had brought long, sunny, hot spells.

Pedalling ahead, I pulled off for the outhouses at the Parker Ridge parking lot, where less than twenty-four hours earlier we'd hiked in short sleeves. A tourist rolled down the window of his rental car. Motioning to the spectacular snow-coated mountains, he asked me, "Are you ready for this?" "No worries," I replied laughing. "I live out here!" "Is this normal?" he asked. "It is at this elevation!" I assured him.

Riding up behind me, Bill, a former shot-put champ who weighed more than 250 pounds and was impervious to cold, was wearing the same thing he did every day – gym shorts and bare legs.

"This is my kind of vacation," he beamed as I hunched my chin into my multiple jacket layers, fully prepared for the long, chilly Big Bend descent.

> LOCALS' LORE: *One fine summer afternoon in June 1898, Banff resident*
> *Christina Alexander hopped on her bicycle dressed in the very proper*
> *attire of the day – an ankle-length skirt – and pedalled 25 kilometres*
> *(15.5 miles) all the way from Banff to Canmore. Riding alongside her*
> *husband on the rutted Canadian Pacific Railway road, Alexander*
> *earned her place in the history books as the first woman to cycle that*
> *route. In the summer of 2010, the Banff Legacy Trail was paved to*
> *provide a multi-use trail running parallel with – but safely separate*
> *from – the Trans-Canada Highway between Canmore and Banff.*

Forty-five minutes farther along, just past Rampart Creek, I was puzzled to notice that all the young trees lining the roadside ditch were standing in about a metre (3 feet) of water. Then, after a few dozen metres, I spied the culprit: a beaver dam only 20 metres (65 feet) from the road, its dome larger than a Volkswagen Beetle. The flooding continued along the roadside for more than a kilometre (0.6 mile). Peter told me later that the beaver dam was a new attraction that summer. He would know. He guides this tour six times a season.

It was Peter's turn to pedal that day, while Dieter drove the van and prepared lunch. Peter told me how when he was fifteen, he had cycled around Europe for two weeks with his parents and his ten-year-old sister, the whole family making sure to be settled near a TV by dinnertime to watch the 1982 soccer World Cup. On his first cycling trip to Canada, Peter biked from Calgary to Vancouver, then down the Pacific Coast to San Francisco. Like so many before him, he fell in love with the Canadian Rockies on that trip, and after living in Vancouver for four years he decided to make a big career change and bought an existing bike tour company. For Dieter's fiftieth birthday, Peter bought his father his first mountain bike, maintaining the cycling ties that bind the family like a lovingly oiled chain.

Sitting in our plastic deck chairs at a pullout overlooking

the Howse River, devouring a feast of hot cider, tomato soup, Caesar salad and pizza, I realized I'd never stopped at that spot before either.

At 95 kilometres (59 miles), this would be our longest day and we were only halfway through it. Before starting out that morning, Peter had coached us, suggesting, "If you want to ride the whole Icefields Parkway, today is the day you can leave it all out there."

The final 8-kilometre (5-mile) climb to Bow Summit took each of us well over an hour, and not everyone was able to complete it, as Bill chose to ride the support van. It was then I realized this was the perfect group vacation for varying degrees of fitness. Those who wanted to ride would certainly get their legs and lungs full at their own pace, while those who decided they'd had enough could sit back and enjoy the chauffeured view. By then I'd also realized that, every single day, Peter had taught me something new about my own Rockies backyard.

Our hotel for the night, Num-Ti-Jah Lodge, set on the shore of robin's-egg-blue Bow Lake, was a fascinating delight, as the walls and floors of this 1920s art deco living museum were, from time-to-time, wonderfully creaky.

From Num-Ti-Jah the next morning everyone chose to pedal, despite the cool Rockies rain. Feeling wet and cold pretty quickly, only thirty minutes after setting out I ducked into the parking lot outhouses at Mosquito Creek Campground to add some layers. Now far behind the others, I rode the next hour by myself, wet and cold, pedalling steadily to keep myself warm. While I did wonder if maybe I should have chosen the van ride that day, I was grateful for all my outdoor experience that had taught me how to handle the weather with both my body and my mind. But then, I wasn't worried. I knew it would be a short day and we'd arrive at Deer Lodge in Lake Louise by early afternoon, where I could gratefully soak in the rooftop Jacuzzi. Marvelling at the familiar mountain landscape, the peaks looked like ghosts, only bits and pieces of them sneaking out from behind wafting cigar-smoke clouds.

Seeing a car stopped on the shoulder, I slowed down, certain they'd spotted some wildlife. As I rolled up closer to the car, I looked in the direction their heads were craning out their partially open window. I spotted it right away – a shiny-wet black bear. Moving deliberately through willows, his big black body parted the glistening green bushes effortlessly. As I slowed down a bit more to have a better look, my brakes squeaked. I could only see parts of the bear's body through the bushes, and not his head, but I could see that he had stopped moving and was looking in my direction – the direction of the squeak. Satisfied that I was no threat, or perhaps just not worth the bother, he lumbered on deeper into the woods, leaving me utterly amazed and enthralled at how easily an animal so large could so quickly make himself utterly invisible. For a moment I'd forgotten how cold and uncomfortable I was, but by the time I reached the van at the Herbert Lake parking lot I was shivering. Huddling in the heated van, I changed into dry clothes and gratefully accepted the hot cider Peter handed me.

I hadn't been bored for a minute.

Best season: The season for cycling the Icefields Parkway can run from early June thru September, depending on your tolerance for cold fingers and toes. No matter what the conditions on the day you begin any multi-day trip in the Rockies, however, you'll always want to pack a toque, gloves, warm layer and rain jacket. If you do see a bear or any other wild animal, NEVER approach it. Snap off a quick photo and continue on your way immediately without disturbing any wildlife. Show respect for them in their home.

Launch point: Having cycled the Icefields Parkway in both directions, I must recommend riding from north to south, Jasper to Banff. With so many of the mountains' glaciated faces being their north-facing ones – the cold, less sunny aspect that permits glaciers to exist – cycling southward presents a steady show of tumbling glaciers for much of the distance. While there are plenty of campsites and several hostels to stay at no matter which direction you choose, if you prefer hotels, then north to south provides the best spacing between wonderful accommodations. To rent a bike in Banff, visit www. snowtips-bactrax.com. To rent one in Jasper, visit www.freewheeljasper.com. For Canmore, go to www.trailsports.ab.ca. Topo map *Banff & Jasper*, www. gemtrek.com.

Banff: Vermilion Lakes Drive, 4.5 kilometres (2.8 miles), no elevation gain, high point 1383 metres (4,537 feet).

For a pleasant, short ride with opportunities for spotting wildlife including bald eagles, osprey, beaver and bighorn sheep, pedal out to Vermilion Lakes Drive. Pack a picnic lunch; there are plenty of places to stop for a leisurely break. Bring binoculars!

Jasper: Take Lodge Road to Lake Edith or Lake Annette, 5 kilometres (3 miles), no elevation gain, high point 1062 metres (3,484 feet).

Follow Connaught Drive east, then cross Highway 16 and the bridge onto Lodge Road. Turn left onto Maligne Road for Lake Edith or follow Lodge Road right for Lake Annette. Don't forget a picnic lunch and your camera!

Banff: Bow Valley Parkway to Lake Louise 58 kilometres (36 miles).

This rolling, paved route provides an outstanding ride along a secondary road where vehicle traffic is slower and the scenery is outstanding, with plentiful possibilities of spotting wildlife, including elk, deer and bears.

Lake Louise: Moraine Lake Road, 15 kilometres (9.3 miles), 335 metres (1,099 feet) elevation gain, high point 1885 metres (6,184 feet).

Jasper: Highway 93A to Athabasca Falls/Highway 93 and 93A junction, 30 kilometres (18.6 miles).

Follow Highway 93 out of Jasper, heading south. At the 7-kilometre (4.3-mile) point, turn right onto Highway 93A. This quiet road offers plenty of viewpoints, occasionally running parallel to the fast-flowing Athabasca River.

While much of the road is bordered by spruce forest, the views that open up at occasional viewpoints are stupendous. Rent a bike from Wilson Mountain Sports, http://wmsll.com.

Jasper to Banff: 289 kilometres (178 miles), high point 2069 metres (6,788 feet).

Cycling the Icefields Parkway is without doubt one of the BEST bike tours in the world, hands-down. If you're fit, and happy to carry panniers, you can cover the distance comfortably in three days, staying at campsites or wilderness hostels along the way. But why rush? You can take time for side hikes if you stretch it out to four or five days. Most campsites are available on a first-come, first-served basis. Check out www.pc.gc.ca and www.hihostels.ca.

To travel light, you can book a room at:

Sunwapta Falls Resort, www.sunwapta.com;

Glacier View Inn overlooking the Columbia Icefield, www.explorerockies.com;

The Crossing Resort at Saskatchewan River Crossing, www.thecrossingresort.com; and

Num-Ti-Jah Lodge, www.num-ti-jah.com.

For the perfect family vacation with teenagers, join a guided – and fully supported – Icefields cycling tour, where a minivan will get you up the hills your legs don't want to, and someone else can do the cooking and the dishes! Check out www.rockymountaincycle.com or www.backroads.com.

Think you have quads of titanium? Try cycling the entire 289-kilometre (180-mile) Icefields Parkway in a single day. Then sign up for your nearest Ironman, 'cause you're worthy!

Wisdom's Trail

"This would be a bad place to fall," Ed Struzik commented casually as Dillon, the horse he was riding, followed close on the hooves of Wisdom, upon whose broad back I was seated.

He was right. The narrow track wound gradually up a steep and rocky side slope with an especially deep, turbulent braid of the Whirlpool River flowing about 10 metres (33 feet) below us to the right.

Struzik was teasing me, because just a few hours earlier, while Greg Horne, a Jasper National Park backcountry warden, had adjusted the stirrups on Wisdom's saddle to fit the legs of my five-foot-four frame, Wisdom had thrust up her head, kicked her forelegs into the air, stepped backward and the next thing I knew I saw stars and felt pain as I hit the ground and more pain as the back half of the horse landed on my leg.

"It happened so fast," I sputtered.

"Looked like a good six seconds to me," Darro Stinson had joked. "If you had just stayed on two seconds longer…"

Fortunately, the soft ground had absorbed my fall and the substantial weight of the horse. And also fortunately, Stinson, a former national park superintendent, was a competent and commanding horseman. He walked Wisdom, with me in her

Jasper National Park wardens Gord Antoniuk and Greg Horne secure a load on a pack horse en route to Athabasca Pass.

saddle, around the campsite, offering a few valuable pointers. Gently pull on the left rein to turn left, likewise on the right, back to stop, not up.

"Power steering," Stinson said. "That's all, power steering."

For the next few hours, our train of ten pack horses and nine saddle horses had crossed river flats, charged up steep banks and sauntered down roller-coaster hills on rock-strewn, muddy sections of the moss-blanketed forest. I'd become quite comfortable with Wisdom's gait and had come to like the way she chose her steps carefully on the rutted trail criss-crossed with tree roots. Given an option, she'd choose the high line with steady footing while the other horses – particularly the young, overeager males – slipped on rocks and sloshed through gooey mud.

But now we were on the most exposed and dangerous section of the trail and the unthinkable happened.

Wisdom slipped.

First her front hooves clacked in desperation to gain purchase on the smooth, down-sloping limestone slab. She lurched forward, her back legs in frantic motion as we pitched to the left, then to the right above the freezing, fast-moving water.

If Wisdom were to fall on me on the way down this steep, rocky bank it would be very bad for both of us.

Then it was over. As quickly as she'd lost her footing, she regained it and we nonchalantly continued up the narrow trail away from the surging river, both of us heaving a sigh of relief.

The expedition had begun at the Moab Lake trailhead in Jasper National Park, our group of eleven people and nineteen horses following the Whirlpool for two days and 41 kilometres (25.5 miles) to Kane Meadows. Named after the nineteenth-century painter Paul Kane, the campsite would serve as a base while four of us set off to climb Mount Brown, a broad, glaciated mountain rising to 2799 metres (9,180 feet) on the west side of Athabasca Pass.

But this was no ordinary climbing trip.

Organized by Bob Sandford in his capacity as coordinator for the United Nations International Year of Mountains Canadian celebrations, the entourage for this six-day, late-August trip included Jasper National Park superintendent Ron Hooper, Jasper backcountry manager Gord Antoniuk and park horse wrangler Sean Elliott. It also included Glenn Charron, manager of the Jasper Yellowhead Museum; Ed Struzik, a journalist from Edmonton; Dave Pors, who represented the Alberta sections of the Alpine Club of Canada; our cook, Liz Norwell; plus Darro Stinson, Greg Horne and me.

The 2002 International Year of Mountains had been declared at the 1992 Earth Summit in Rio de Janeiro, when mountain regions worldwide were formally recognized as important planetary water towers and repositories of biodiversity and cultural heritage. The Rio summit also formally recognized that mountain ecosystems worldwide face challenges as important as desertification, climate change and tropical deforestation. While many of Canada's most cherished mountain areas may appear to be well protected by national and provincial park designations, their ecosystems face many of the same threats as mountain regions in less-developed countries. The pressures exerted by heavy visitation and urban growth in areas bordering protected lands affect the capacity for those sensitive regions to be managed effectively. Canada's protected lands may not be as well protected as many would like to think.

Our trip to Athabasca Pass was designed to help draw attention to the importance of Canada's mountain areas with the hope that the more people become aware of the unique, fragile and valuable resources found in those mountains, the more people will care about preserving them.

For four decades following explorer David Thompson's first recorded crossing in 1811, Athabasca Pass remained the main fur trade route through the Canadian Rockies. In May 1827, while travelling with Hudson's Bay Company traders and voyageurs, a young Scottish botanist named David Douglas tightened his snowshoe laces and plodded his way up the glaciated slopes of the peak west of the pass. Pleased with his endeavour, he named the mountain after an illustrious British botanist named Robert Brown and attributed heights of 4900 metres (16,000 feet) and 5200 metres (17,000 feet) respectively to Brown and nearby Mount Hooker. In doing so, Douglas was claiming these mountains to be – by far – the highest in North America.

Douglas was a botanist, not a surveyor, however, and was famously poor-sighted to boot. Still, while travelling some 16,000 kilometres (9,900 miles) through the remote western Canadian mountain landscape, he did manage to identify an astounding 880 species of plants, 200 of which were new to science, including his namesake Douglas fir. The heights he assigned to Brown and Hooker were outrageously generous, but it is possible Douglas believed Athabasca Pass rested at 3355 metres (11,007 feet), based on an incorrect map that had been published prior to his visit.

The prospect of climbing such colossal mountains in the Canadian wilderness lured many accomplished mountaineers for decades afterward in a race to be the first to claim their prize summits. Though it would not be until 1893 that University of Toronto geologist A.P. Coleman would prove that mounts Brown and Hooker were only a disappointing 2801 and 3307 metres (9,190 and 10,850 feet) respectively, in the meantime much was accomplished in exploring and mapping the uncharted Canadian Rockies in pursuit of the mystery peaks.

As I rocked gently with Wisdom's movements as she felt out the slippery riverbed rocks in the Whirlpool's silty, fast-moving, smoky-blue water that rose close to her sagging belly, I thought about how little of this remote and rugged mountain landscape had changed over the past two centuries. While glaciers tumbling from mounts Kane and Scott have retreated high above treeline, fresh wolf, moose and bear tracks appeared frequently in the mud. The only other people we encountered in six days were five American hikers, coincidentally pursuing their annual pilgrimage of following a segment of Douglas's travels.

Other than the luxury of established trails, the physical labour of a horse trip hasn't changed much, either, since Douglas first travelled the route. With the help of Stinson, Horne, Antoniuk and Hooper, Elliot looked after nineteen horses: replacing horseshoes, securing loads, checking legs for injuries and hobble burn and riding bareback in the hazy predawn light to round up the spirited steeds after their night's grazing in lush meadows to saddle them all up for another day's travel. At mealtime Norwell made sure we feasted on such backcountry delights as pasta and salad, cornbread and roast beef, all cooked over open fires.

On the third day, all eleven of us hiked to a pair of jewel-toned lakes planted at the crest of Athabasca Pass that mark the divide between the Pacific and Arctic watersheds. Sandford described how one of the lakes, now known as the Committee's Punchbowl, was where fur traders would stop and drink a toast to the officers of the Hudson's Bay Company. We too stopped there to toast the Committee and also Douglas with some rum, and to enjoy a refreshing dip. Then Horne, Pors, Elliot and I embarked on our climb.

No doubt equipped with better clothing and footwear than Douglas had been, the four of us made our way up through meadows and talus benches, crunching over scree and through rock bands and short cliffs, finally following a snow ramp until we found the perfect high camp. With a 270-degree view and protected by a low rock wall, our strategic location would allow us quick access to the summit the following morning. It also sheltered us from the wind that accompanied booming thunder and lightning flashes and vigorous rains that evening.

Shortly before 11 a.m. on August 30 we reached the summit cairn, which sat quietly amid a dozen or so perfectly round craters, each about half a metre across and half that deep, set in the shale-strewn plateau. The craters looked as if a giant had punched his fist into the mountaintop, and we wondered if they might have been created by lightning. Inside a tightly capped plastic tube wedged into the cairn, we found the soggy register notebook that had last been signed in 1993 by seasoned Rockies climbers Glen Boles, Rollie Reader and Mike Budd, testimony to the relative present-day obscurity of a mountain that had once been sought after by the world's best mountaineers. On that day, the summit view coveted by all mountaineers

Sean Elliott, Dave Pors and Greg Horne examine the summit register on Mount Brown.

LOCALS' LORE: *Marked by a cairn, the Committee's Punchbowl is a small lake at the summit of Athabasca Pass marking the Continental Divide, from which water flows toward both the Pacific and the Arctic oceans. The Punchbowl was named by Governor George Simpson in reference to the London Committee of the Hudson's Bay Company. During the four decades the pass served as the main fur trade route across the Canadian Rockies, linking Canada and the Oregon country, the traders would stop at the lake and toast the Committee with a dram of rum.*

Kane Meadows was named for Canadian artist Paul Kane, who travelled over the pass in 1846 as part of a two-year expedition from Toronto to Fort Victoria on the Pacific Coast. His watercolour paintings and sketches chronicled life in the Canadian West prior to the invention of photography.

was not to be ours and we descended through cloud and fog along the sometimes technical northeast ridge. Lower down we endured a section of bushwhacking much like Douglas might have seen, where we were grateful to discover a profusion of ripe huckleberry bushes. Grabbing handfuls of delectable berries as we plodded downhill prevented the steep descent through thick, rain-slick alders from being entirely heinous.

Back at the campfire that night we celebrated our climb and also Douglas's, and repeatedly toasted the serendipity of his great mistake and the splendour of the Canadian Rockies. We also raised our camping cups of single malt or Caribbean rum enthusiastically to the luxury of having horses to carry such treats to our home base among such remote peaks.

In the spirit of clever fun and historical re-enactment, those members of our expedition who had remained at base camp while we climbers were on the mountain had arranged for a mock inquiry to be staged. Wearing a saddle cinch over his head to resemble (just barely) a magistrate's wig, Hooper presided over the campfire court as Justice. Charron sat quietly on a tree stump in the role of Douglas, accused of lying about his ascent and exaggerating the heights of mounts Brown and Hooker for his own personal gain. Struzik took to his role as prosecutor like a starving dog to a T-bone; Stinson filled the defence's shoes with off-the-cuff aplomb. One by one the four climbers were called to the stand as witnesses to the validity of Douglas's reported ascent and descent times, his recordings of plant life above treeline and the possibility that much more extensive glaciation would have allowed him to climb a very different Mount Brown than we were now doing in 2002. With a rope neatly knotted into a noose lying unceremoniously on the ground, anyone stumbling upon this crepuscular scene two days' hike from the nearest road might have headed quickly for more distant hills. In the end, Hooper found Douglas to be innocent on both charges, though he chastised the botanist for his atrocious altitude-estimating abilities.

Despite its imperfections, Douglas's ascent of Mount Brown is considered the birth of North American mountaineering. Our expedition marked one in a series of commemorative climbs in 2002 celebrating the Year of Mountains. In May, Parks Canada wardens climbed an unnamed peak in Auyuittuq National Park in southern Baffin Island, where they unfurled an International Year of Mountains flag on the summit to celebrate more than fifty years of organized rescue services in Canada's national parks. The following month, another group of wardens participating in regular training camps climbed two 3048-metre (10,000-foot) peaks in the front ranges of Yukon's St. Elias Mountains. While they were there, they restored a maple leaf that had been created of white rocks on a slope above their camp in the Steele Valley by participants in the Alpine Club of Canada's 1967 centennial camp, where a dozen peaks first climbed that year in honour of the country's 100th birthday were named after deceased ACC presidents.

Then, in July, climbers marked the centennial of the first ascent of 3747-metre (12,293-foot) Mount Columbia, Alberta's highest peak and the second highest in the Canadian Rockies.

Two separate teams participated, one comprised of park wardens on a training exercise, the other a party of three clients led by a Yamnuska Mountain Adventures guide.

As I crawled into my sleeping bag on the last night of our trip, I felt completely intoxicated by my surroundings and the pleasure of my companions' acquaintance. Travelling by horse train provided an enchanting richness that I had not experienced on any other kind of mountain trip. I felt transported through time, as if I had become part of the landscape, so that I was not simply moving through it but participating in its very existence. The landscape and I had merged. Time also had merged. I felt bad for unprepared young brides who had been forced by their fur-trading husbands to endure the hardships of mountain travel, all the while expected to raise children in a physically and spiritually challenging landscape.

But then I felt camaraderie with those women who came to this mountain wilderness early in the twentieth century, educated and independent women who found their spirits in these mountains and who chose not to return to their former urban homes. I was lulled into a land of sweet, earthy dreams by the faint tinkling of the horses' bells as they munched contentedly in the riverside pasture, and in that moment I understood fully the allure that drew Douglas and many others before and since to explore the unique and miraculous landscapes of the Canadian Rockies and summits real and imagined.

Best seasons: The two-day hike to Athabasca Pass is a quiet walk in big wilderness during the summer months. It's a bit more remote and isolated a destination for experienced, hardy backcountry skiers who relish winter camping so far from pavement and a hot shower! But if wilderness solitude makes your heart sing, this destination will have you competing with the most melodious songbirds.

Trailhead: Follow the Icefields Parkway to Athabasca Falls, 31 kilometres (19.3 miles) south of Jasper townsite, and turn west onto Highway 93A. Follow 93A north for 9 kilometres (5.6 miles) to the Moab Lake access road junction. Follow Moab Lake Road for 7 kilometres (4.4 miles) to the parking area. Topo maps *Athabasca Falls 83 C/12*, *Amethyst Lakes 83 D/9*, *Athabasca Pass 83 D/8*. (Note: the last 36 kilometres, (22.4 miles), are not marked on the maps.)

Moab Lake is just a short walk from the parking lot, but the restored fire road continuing up the valley offers pleasant walking for the next 8.5 kilometres (5.3 miles) before it reverts to a rocky, rooty and often muddy horse trail. Pack a lunch and bring a backcountry camp chair and a good book!

Scott Camp Campground, 30.9 kilometres (19.2 miles), 115 metres (377 feet) elevation gain, high point 1325 metres (4,347 feet). Camp at Simon Creek the first night, 15 kilometres (9.3 miles).

If you don't have the time or energy to make the trip all the way to Athabasca Pass, the view of Scott Glacier – a tongue of the Hooker Icefield – from the Whirlpool River gravel flats makes for a very rewarding three- to four-day destination.

Athabasca Pass, 49 kilometres (30.5 miles), elevation gain 545 metres (1,780 feet), high point 1755 metres (5,758 feet). Mount Brown, 2799 metres (9,183 feet).

If there's one backcountry historical place worth visiting, Athabasca Pass, first crossed by explorer extraordinaire David Thompson in 1811 – led by his guide, Thomas the Iroquois – is it, purely for the romance of inhaling the spirits of those extraordinarily hardy men who travelled through there for the nearly half-century the route served as the Rockies' major fur trade route. Spend your first night at Middle Forks Campground, 21 kilometres (13 miles), and the second night at either Kane Meadows, 41 kilometres

(25.5 miles) or Committee's Punchbowl campground, 48.5 kilometres (30 miles). Give yourself the time to climb Mount Brown and enjoy the view!

Hiking and Biking: Whirlpool River, 8.5 kilometres (5.3 miles) to Tie Camp warden cabin.

The fire road section of this trail makes for an excellent mountain bike excursion, complete with fabulous views of Mount Edith Cavell. If you're keen on a night of camping, you can stash your bike and hike another 3.8 kilometres (2.4 miles) to Tie Camp Campground. From this place, in the early 1900s, timber was floated down the Whirlpool to the Athabasca River and all the way to Jackladder, near Jasper, where the logs were made into railway ties. To lengthen your ride, start at the Highway 93A junction – particularly enjoyable in the winter off-season when the road is closed to vehicles. Phone 780.852.6176.

Hire a guide: If you don't have the requisite skills and experience, or you want to improve the skills you do have, hire a guide to take you on any of these adventures or to organize a custom trip: www.acmg. ca, www.yamnuska.com or www.internationalguidebureau.com.

A Log Jewel in the Wilderness

The first time I hiked into the Tonquin Valley in Jasper National Park, my friend Gail Johns and I followed the Astoria River trail through dense trees until it branched up steep switchbacks on the south slope of Old Horn Mountain. Just as we started to wonder whether the switchbacks would ever end, the trail levelled out on the west slope of Old Horn, and there it was, right in front of us like a real-life IMAX experience: the Tonquin Valley. The jewel-toned waters of the two Amethyst Lakes glimmered delicately at the base of the towering black rock wall of The Ramparts. The scale of the valley was so immense I imagined dropping the entire town of Banff into the basin and having it all but disappear.

After 24 kilometres (15 miles) of hiking with heavy, multi-day packs, we had a similar impression on seeing Wates-Gibson Hut, one of the Alpine Club of Canada's majestic log cabins. As we dragged our tired feet and butts up the relentlessly inclined final 500 metres (550 yards), we saw it – a large, stately log building tucked behind a screen of spruce trees bordering the still, pewter-coloured waters of Outpost Lake. The hut stood like a true jewel in the wilderness, much like the nearby Amethyst Lakes.

That first trip took place in late September, when the trail was firm and dry, the air crisp and the advancing north wind was pushing the spruces and firs back and forth between fall and winter. The first night, we shared the hut with three others, who hiked off in the morning, leaving the two of us alone with Speedy, the resident packrat. Between cold rain showers we hiked along the moraine of the Fraser Glacier above the hut, retreating to the woodstove and steaming cups of tea as dark, pre-winter skies advanced.

In *The Canadian Rockies Trail Guide*, authors Brian Patton and Bart Robinson quote nineteenth-century explorer J. Monroe Thorington, who was so impressed by the Tonquin that he wrote how its "unique combination of lake, precipice, and ice … presents itself with a singular beauty almost unequalled in alpine regions of North America." Patton and Robinson admit that late in the season this may very well be so, but then include the following caution: "In the midst of summer, when the rains are pelting down, the mosquitoes and black flies and no-see-ums are swarming … the trails have been churned to mush by heavy horse use, this lovely area comes very close to a backpacker's definition of hell."

And so, on my second trip into the area, I joined past ACC president Mike Mortimer, long-time club member and legendary Rockies climber Glen Boles, Alpine Club staffers Nancy Hansen and Leslie de Marsh, and Fern Heitkamp, who would work tirelessly as our cook, on the third leg of a "Taste of the Rockies" tour, designed to dazzle visiting members of the American Alpine Club, the Dutch Mountaineering Association and the International Mountaineering and Climbing Federation, or UIAA (*Union internationale des associations d'alpinisme*). It was mid-July, and to be fair I don't remember having much of a problem with black flies or no-see-ums. As for the mud and the mosquitoes, those were unforgettable.

One of the biggest reasons people choose to hike and climb is to explore the natural environment, and for the most part they accept the potential for discomfort in doing so. The reward, of course, comes not from enjoying the experience despite the weather, but from embracing whatever weather as part of the experience.

And so, while stepping through one oozing mud puddle to the next we marvelled at the perfect moose prints and wondered how far away the moose was. Green gentians, lacelike grass of Parnassus and brilliant fuchsia river beauties lined the Astoria River trail (at 17 kilometres, or 10.6 miles, much shorter than my earlier route) all the way to Chrome Lake. Outings in inclement weather provide plenty of time for philosophical discussions such as "when the weather report says there's a thirty per cent chance of rain, does that mean it will only rain thirty per cent of the day or that there's a thirty per cent chance it will rain where you are? Or does it mean the clouds will only dump thirty per cent of their load for 100 per cent of the day while the mosquitoes suck thirty per cent of your blood?"

The hut, thank goodness, was warm, dry and mosquito free. After a comforting dinner of pasta with fresh salad and plenty of wine, Ernst, editor of the UIAA *Journal*, who hails from a village in the Bavarian Alps, explained the hoofed species of Canadian wildlife to me. In the German language, he said, a moose is an elk and an elk is a red deer. I asked if that wasn't a caribou? No, he replied, a caribou is a reindeer. Mammoths, he declared, are still mammoths. I believed him. Ernst also told me how some huts in the Bavarian Alps can accommodate 350 people, swelling to 600 on holidays. Wates-Gibson can sleep thirty, so we were very comfortable with our group of sixteen, placing two long tables together for a big L-shaped dinner table. It pleased me to notice how we came to feel so at home in such a short time.

We woke the next morning to the sound of rain drumming on the roof. Without newspapers or e-mail, nobody minded spending the morning drinking tea and coffee and enjoying leisurely conversation. By noon a crack of sunshine had slipped through the clouds and lit up the puddles outside the front door. As if on cue, everyone was suddenly busy, making lunches, packing raingear and lacing boots. Glen Boles led ten of us on a right and proper bushwhack through the forest below Surprise Point. Glen had climbed about 600 mountains over the course of forty-five years, 475 of them in the Canadian Rockies.

"I was really lucky. I climbed with all good guys, all better climbers than me," he told me. I thought he must have held his own on the rope while putting up new routes on Mount Edith Cavell, Deltaform and the Hourglass on Robson. Glen could name nearly every peak in the Tonquin the group asked him about.

Nearly two hours later, we arrived at the Surprise Point campsite, resting for lunch in the meadow. One of the group spotted a bald eagle, soaring and spiralling in thermals against a backdrop of Mount Clitheroe's velvety green lower slopes.

Reindert, president of the Dutch Mountaineering Association, and his wife, Irene, couldn't help but appreciate the scale of the landscape. "It's overwhelming," Reindert said. "It's totally another scale. Everything is much bigger than the Alps. Wherever you go in the Alps, there are people. In Europe there are no quiet places."

LOCALS' LORE: *Mount Edith Cavell was named in 1916 in honour of a British nurse during the First World War who was in charge of a unit whose main purpose was to help soldiers trapped behind enemy lines rejoin their outfits. The Germans considered this an act of treason, and executed her. Wates-Gibson Hut also has ties to the Great War, as some of the money that enabled the hut to be built came from the Alpine Club of Canada's Soldier's Memorial Fund, which was set up in the early years of the club in remembrance of Canadians who gave their lives in the 1914–18 conflict. The current structure is actually the third to be built in that location; the original was built in 1930, its replacement in 1947 and the present hut in 1962. Cyril Wates served as ACC president from 1938 to 1941; Rex Gibson, a veteran of both world wars, was serving his second term as ACC president at the time of his death in a climbing accident in 1957.*

Gail Crowe-Swords soaks in the spectacular view of The Ramparts while skiing in to the Alpine Club of Canada's Wates-Gibson Hut in Jasper's Tonquin Valley.

Geographically smaller than Nova Scotia, the Netherlands has a population of 16.6 million.

"For us Dutch people, this is amazing. I think we must do this," added Irene. We hiked the trail back to the hut, content to have been outside for nearly four hours without getting rained on.

The first hut in the Eremite Valley was built in 1930 on the north side of Penstock Creek, a memorial to climbers who had died in the Canadian mountains and those who had given their lives in the First World War. Poorly sited on swampy ground, the building's foundation collapsed. It was replaced by a log structure on the north shore of Outpost Lake in honour of Cyril G. Wates, who served as Alpine Club of Canada president from 1938 to 1941. Built too small and too close to the lake, the original Wates hut was in turn replaced with a much larger one in 1962, with a dedication that included Rex Gibson, who served as ACC president from 1954 to 1957. The present location offers easy access to Thunderbolt, Outpost and Angle peaks, Anchorite, Mount Erebus, and Alcove Mountain as well as the Eremite Group, with more not far away. You could stay here a month and still feel like you were just getting started.

Snacking on pâté and caviar and sipping red wine, the group, whose members had met only a week earlier, carried on various conversations that blended seamlessly into the night air, softened by the glow of candlelight and the warmth of the woodstove. George Gluck, a director of the American Alpine Club, told me about his passion, the Volunteers in Parks program. For more than fifty years he's spent time at Yosemite, a place for which he declares his unconditional love. He and his volunteers tackle the "shit jobs," including trail maintenance and ash removal from campsites following forest fires.

Everyone in the hut recognized the opportunity to learn from one another, sharing ideas on land use issues and liability challenges, expressing a mutual caring and love for the mountain world and the pursuit of encouraging people to enjoy it. The various directors of national alpine clubs expressed a mutual desire to discover what they could do for their members and how to attract members who might ask what they could do for their club.

Looking around the hut, I knew the scene was one that hadn't changed in decades. No cell phones, no laptops, no TV. People sat talking, sharing their similarities and learning from their differences in the universal language of the mountains.

Best season: Like many Rockies destinations, Jasper National Park's Tonquin Valley is quite a bit more accessible in the summer than once the trails are buried in snow. On top of that, Edith Cavell Road, which provides motor vehicle access to the start of the shortest hiking route into the area, is not plowed in winter. Even in summer, however, this narrow, winding road is off-limits to large motorhomes and trailers, though those can be parked in a large lot at the base of the road.

Trailhead: From Jasper, drive south on the Icefields Parkway for 6.8 kilor̄ (4.2 miles), then turn right onto Highway 93A. Drive south for 5.5 kilometre̊ (3.4 miles) to the junction with Edith Cavell Road. Follow that for 13.5 kilometres (8.4 miles), and park in the parking lot that marks the end of the road, just beyond Cavell Lake. Topo map *Amethyst Lakes 83 D/9*.

Cavell Pond interpretive trail, 1.8 kilometres (1.1 miles) loop trail, gradual minor elevation gain, high point 1750 metres (5,742 feet).

There are few places in the world where you can walk right up and stick your hands into a glacier pool and watch mini-icebergs calve off and splash into the water a safe distance away. This spot is a gem. Dress warm, though; it will be much cooler at the base of Mount Edith Cavell than in downtown Jasper.

Cavell Meadows, 8.3 kilometres (5.2 miles) loop trail, 370 metres (1,214 feet) elevation gain, high point 2288 metres (7,507 feet).

For a hike with a real view to remember, pack a lunch and a warm layer and head up the trail to Cavell Meadows. Bring your camera to capture stunning views of Mount Edith Cavell and Angel Glacier dropping into the pool at its base, as well as the kaleidoscope of wildflowers carpeting the meadows. Be sure to check with Parks Canada at 780.852.6176 to make sure the trail is open if you're planning to hike before mid-July.

A Log Jewel

Wates-Gibson Hut, Chrome Lake–Eremite Valley trail, 19 kilometres (11.8 miles), 180 metres (591 feet) elevation gain, high point 1900 metres (6,234 feet).

The shortest route to Wates-Gibson Hut follows the Astoria River, then branches left at the 8.2-kilometre (5-mile) point, crossing over a log bridge. The trail stays close to the valley bottom, with little elevation gain except for a steep bit right before the hut. If you're keen on a more scenic route or would prefer to camp at one of the Tonquin Valley's delightful backcountry sites, you can branch right at the bridge rather than cross it, and follow an upper trail to

Clitheroe or Surprise Point campground. See *The Canadian Rockies Trail Guide*, by Brian Patton and Bart Robinson.

Mount Edith Cavell, 3363 metres (11,033 feet), East Ridge, III, 5.3.

   This blocky quartzite ridge on a beautiful, symmetrical mountain is one of the classic alpine climbs of the Canadian Rockies. If you've got the experience, check out the full route description in *The 11,000ers of the Canadian Rockies*, by Bill Corbett.

Cross-country skiing: Edith Cavell Road is not plowed in the winter, but it is track-set, making for excellent cross-country skiing. Park in the lot at the base of the road and start skiing!

Ski touring: Most backcountry skiers heading for Wates-Gibson Hut ski as far as the HI-Edith Cavell Wilderness Hostel, www.hihostels.ca, the first night, and continue up the Astoria River to the hut the second day. While this is not a destination for ultra-long, steep and deep backcountry skiing, the Tonquin Valley offers a multitude of options for moderate ski tours. For an alternative route, ski to Amethyst Lakes via Maccarib Pass, accessed by Marmot Basin Road. For a full route description, see *Ski Trails in the Canadian Rockies*, by Chic Scott.

Hire a guide: If you don't have the requisite skills and experience, or you want to improve the skills you do have, hire a guide to take you on any of these adventures or to organize a custom trip: www.acmg.ca, www.yamnuska.com or www.internationalguidebureau.com.

Ski Adventure Leaves More To Come

"Hi, I'm Mike," said the man stepping out of the minivan, extending his hand. "Man, I'm feeling like crap this morning, my kid kept me up all night with the flu."

Returning the handshake, I was glad to be wearing gloves and decided that of all the greetings I've shared with new trip partners, this was not my favourite. Apparently, I was about to embark on a four-day ski traverse with someone whose toddler had just slobbered flu germs all over him. Worse, we would be sharing a very small backpacking tent for three nights.

There were four of us on this trip: Mike, me, and Jackie and Steve Fedyna, who would share their own tent. Our plan was to ski the Six Pass route in Jasper National Park, linking high alpine passes up and down from one valley to the next starting from Maligne Lake and finishing 50 kilometres (31 miles) to the south at the Sunwapta warden station at Poboktan Creek. The expedition had been organized by Jackie and Steve in their capacity as volunteer trip leaders with the Alpine Club of Canada's (ACC) Rocky Mountain Section.

The forecast over the Easter long weekend, however, seemed to have other plans, as a storm was scheduled to arrive the following day. But since we'd all been planning this for weeks, all of us were keen to at least give it a try.

Hoisting a pack with four days' food, winter-weight sleeping bags, backpacking cookstoves, fuel and four-season tent parts always comes as a bit of a shock to the body at the parking lot. There is no ignoring that it feels heavy, but at the same time, you know you can't dwell on it. With skins on our skis, we pushed our way slowly up the broad, level and fortunately well-travelled fire road leading to Bald Hills Lookout. Five sluggish kilometres (3.1 miles) and 480 vertical metres (1,575 feet) later, we left the packed trail and headed across the open, windswept plateau, having completed the first of the six passes.

A few winters later, four skiers departed from the Signal Mountain trailhead, fifteen minutes by car from downtown Jasper's Connaught Drive.

For the following nineteen days and nearly 300 kilometres (186 miles), Chic Scott and his companions – Margaret Gmoser, Scott's friend since high school, Colorado river guide Faye Atkinson and Vancouver-based outdoor photographer Tony Hoare – skied with forty-five-pound packs on their backs, camping at night and melting snow to cook over their compact gas stoves.

Laden with five to seven days' food between caches, they followed the Skyline hiking trail. They then linked to the Eight Pass backcountry ski route, pioneered by mountain guide Willie Pfisterer, who was Jasper National Park's first alpine specialist in the late 1960s. For Scott, a veteran of numerous long-distance backcountry ski traverses, it was his first time linking the Signal Mountain to Poboktan Creek section.

"I'm calling that the Thirteen Pass route," Scott said. "That route alone takes about a week and is just as good as the entire Wapta Traverse. It stays up high almost all the time, just with no glaciers – and no huts."

From Poboktan Creek they crossed the Brazeau Icefield, skied over Jonas Pass and through the White Goat Wilderness to reach the David Thompson Highway via the Cline River.

At that point everyone responded positively to Scott's

suggestion they ski out to Nordegg "for a hamburger."

"Not only that, beer too," Gmoser added. "All of us perked right up."

"We got there at day thirteen and we were tired," Scott admitted. "But we weren't quite ready to quit yet."

Having received daily updates from the skiers via a SPOT satellite communication system, Banff's Jeanette Fish and Chuck O'Callaghan decided to surprise the group at their David Thompson food cache. But everyone was surprised when Fish and O'Callaghan spotted Hoare and Gmoser hitchhiking on the side of the road. Not only was the lift to Nordegg appreciated, so were the goodies Fish and O'Callaghan carried, including fresh vegetables.

After soaking in multiple showers and plentiful meals for two nights in Nordegg, the skiers continued up the Siffleur River to Pipestone Creek. They arrived at Skoki Lodge after six days, just in time to celebrate St. Patrick's Day with a group known as the Green Waxers.

"We ended the trip with two days of partying at Skoki," Scott said. "It was nice to sleep in a bed, eat good food and be warm. There, Marg and I decided to pack it in. We'd skied 300 kilometres and Margaret's knees had been hurting for ten days. She never complained; she just motored along."

Hoare and Atkinson continued skiing to Banff via Baker Creek, Pulsatilla Pass and Mystic Pass to Mount Norquay – making Atkinson one of few women to ski the entire Jasper to Banff route.

With 2010 marking the eightieth anniversary of the first ski traverse between Jasper and Banff, Scott said he and his companions planned their trip as a fitting celebration. In 1930, Swiss-born Joe Weiss, who pioneered five massive ski traverses in Jasper and Banff parks between 1929 and 1933, led four others for fifteen days along what is now the Icefields Parkway, reaching Banff in time for the winter carnival. Scott said his group's route, along the parkway's east side, had been skied in

1976 by Donnie Gardner and Larry Mason, the late 1970s by Bob Saunders and Mel Hines and by a group in 1985.

"But I don't think anybody's skied it since," Scott said.

Gmoser, now a grandmother, had raised two sons while her husband, Hans, was running his pioneering heli-ski company, Canadian Mountain Holidays. A fit and experienced back-country skier, she said she appreciated being able to make such a trip in her prime. Gmoser, like Scott, was just months shy of her sixty-fifth birthday at the time of their big traverse.

"I figured, both of us are sixty-five this year," she said. "We're both in shape, so let's go!"

Scott joked that, since the Banff to Lake Louise journey was his tenth major ski traverse in the mountains of western Canada, he "should have known better."

"It was hard work, from the moment we woke up," Scott said of the expedition. "We'd rouse from our slumber and things would be frozen, frost on the tent, our boots were cold. Then all through the day we were constantly making decisions. On glacier trips you can often relax into cruise mode, but on this trip, every twenty seconds you had to make another decision – ski around this log, over this log jam or take your skis off and climb over something.

LOCALS' LORE: *Joe Weiss was a Swiss-born adventurer who settled in western Canada and over the course of five years made five epic ski traverses in Jasper and Banff national parks. His first big traverse was a solo ski from Jasper to the Columbia Icefield, a 200-kilometre (124-mile) round trip. Chic Scott and companions' 2010 trip was planned in part to commemorate the 80th anniversary of the first ski traverse between Jasper and Banff, which Weiss completed in 1930 with four partners. Weiss's group skied for 15 days, following what is now the Icefields Parkway, reaching Banff just in time for the winter carnival.*

"It was a real adventure. This was a big trip, it was full on. I've never been so tired in my life. It was as hard as any trip I've ever done. *Maybe* being older was a factor."

A name now synonymous with Canadian climbing history and mountain writing, Chic Scott is a fourth-generation Albertan. With his father, Charles F. Scott, being a member of the Alberta Sports Hall of Fame, Chic grew up immersed in amateur sports. By 1961 he was a golf prodigy representing Alberta at the Canadian junior championships. The following year, he discovered skiing and mountaineering, and never stopped looking upward.

As a young climber, Scott knew the story of how, in 1960, Hans Gmoser (who married Margaret in 1966), and five others had attempted to ski the high glacier route between Lake Louise and Jasper. After enduring storms, avalanches, crevasse falls, lost food caches, and dissension within the group, they were forced to abort their expedition.

So, in 1967, Scott, Donnie Gardner, Neil Liske and Charlie Locke, set out to complete Gmoser's project. Equipped with Nordic skis and wax imported from Norway, and with carefully placed food caches, the four young Canadians made the first ski traverse to follow the Great Divide from Jasper to Lake Louise, over high alpine passes and across crevasse-wrinkled glaciers. The trip took them twenty-one days and it would be twenty years before anyone replicated it.

"The Great Divide traverse was a pivotal point in the Canadian mountaineering story," Scott explained. "Up until that time, virtually anything of significance accomplished in Canadian mountains had been done by foreigners, except for a few routes on Yamnuska. All the big first ascents, even in the Yukon, had been done by Austrians, Swiss, Brits, Americans, and not home-grown Canadians. For us, there was no doubt in our minds: we were making a Canadian statement."

For Scott it marked the beginning, as he became a key figure in the first wave of Canadian-born climbers to earn their place

From left, Donnie Gardner, Chic Scott, Charlie Locke and Neil Liske savour their success after completing the first-ever 21-day Jasper to Lake Louise glacier ski traverse in 1967. 📷 DON GARDNER

on the international stage of what, until then, had been a British- and European-dominated pursuit.

In the mid-1960s, Scott established new routes on the Rockies' Ship's Prow Buttress and Mount Stephen. At just twenty, he made the first winter ascent of 3493-metre (11,460 foot) Mount Hungabee, and a year later, 1967, the first winter ascent of 3618-metre (11,870-foot) Mount Assiniboine, the Rockies' most serious winter climb at that time. Beginning in 1968, Scott spent five summers in the European Alps, making serious ascents of the range's test-piece routes, including the Gervasutti Pillar on Mont Blanc du Tacul. During summers in those years, he worked for top British climber Dougal Haston's International School of Mountaineering in Leysin, Switzerland, guiding routes on Mont Blanc and the Matterhorn. During his last summer there, Scott worked on the climbing safety team for the Clint Eastwood film *The Eiger Sanction*. Then, in 1973, he joined a British team attempting to climb 7661-metre (25,135-foot) Dhaulagiri IV in Nepal, and in reaching the 6400-metre (21,000-foot) summit of Myagdi Matha, Chic Scott became the first Canadian to climb a Himalayan peak.

Back on home turf, he completed numerous long-distance ski traverses in the Rockies and BC's Selkirks, including the 130-kilometre (81-mile), fifteen-day Rogers Pass to Bugaboos high alpine traverse.

In 1986, Scott's route diverged. The Calgary Mountain Club, which counted Canada's top climbers among its membership, was celebrating its 25th anniversary. As club president, Scott compiled a hefty scrapbook of newspaper clippings and photos and wrote some historical chapters. Unknowingly, he had just begun what would become his life's work. In 1992 he published his first book, *Ski Trails in the Canadian Rockies*, followed in 1994 by *Summits and Icefields*, a dream-list of ski-mountaineering objectives in the Rockies and Columbias, and the first guidebook of its kind. Then, after thirteen years of teaching in the human physiology labs at the University of Calgary, he embraced the mountains full time in 1988. While his popular publications established him as western Canada's premier backcountry ski guidebook author, it was *Pushing the Limits*, published by Rocky Mountain Books, which heralded the arrival of Chic Scott, mountain writer.

"I never set off to be a writer, it just happened," Scott admitted. "But with *Pushing the Limits*, I did set out to diligently record Canadian climbing history. I thought it would take two years, but it just kept growing and growing."

The result was a 440-page, 600-photograph volume covering 200 years of climbing history in Canada, from Labrador's Torngats to Yukon's St. Elias Range to the Pacific Coast Mountains. By the time the book was published, in 2000, Scott had devoted six years to this definitive work.

"My whole life has been about promoting the Canadian mountain experience," Scott said. "In the early days, I actually did it – pioneered new climbing routes and long backcountry ski traverses. I carried the Canadian flag in Europe and in the Himalaya. The theme has always been about our Canadian mountain experience. Any way you look at it – the climbing

and skiing, the personalities and characters and the history –
it's just as good as any nation on earth."

Powder Pioneers followed in 2005, and in 2009 Scott self-
published *Deep Powder and Steep Rock*, a biography of Hans
Gmoser.

And at an age when most are content to prop up their down-
bootie-clad feet by the woodstove, Scott continues to be part of
the story.

The March 2010 ski tour had been on his mind for years.
Blessed with great weather – only one snowy day the entire
trip – the travelling was smooth and enjoyable on the high,
open, windswept passes, but often exhausting lower down.

"In the valley bottoms it was terrible," Scott said. "We had
no rest. We split into teams at the end of the day, one person
shovelling out a cooking area, the other shovelling out tent
pads. After an hour, hour and a half, we'd have a great camp.
Sip of whisky, off to bed, sleep like a rock for ten or eleven
hours, then up into a cold morning again."

The adventure, however, was unforgettable, along with some
of the views.

"We had no navigation problems, no whiteouts – even
though the valley bottoms were the pits," Margaret Gmoser
recounted. "Starting from the north we needed that visibility.
There are some tricky spots and we had to avoid cornices and
ski some steep side slopes. But the [avalanche] stability was
good; there were no naturals [avalanches], no whoomphing.
We felt good about that. And the northern section had some of
the most beautiful mountain scenery anywhere."

Admitting to counting on multiple doses of "vitamin I"
(ibuprofen) to relieve the pain from having had her kneecaps
removed years before, Gmoser said she and Scott owed great
thanks to Atkinson and Hoare.

"I felt bad I couldn't contribute to the trail-breaking, but they
said 'No, we like breaking trail,'" Gmoser said. "I thought I
should call it quits at Nigel Creek, but they convinced me to

Ski Adventure

Author Lynn Martel mugs for the camera in the last rays of evening light while camped on Jasper's Bald Hills summit on the first night of the Six Pass ski route.

LYNN MARTEL COLLECTION

carry on. We could not have done this trip without Faye and Tony. They broke trail the whole way. Our little group of four got along so well. We were tired and cold and wet and hungry but we got along just great. We made group decisions. There was never a cross word.

"It was an awesome trip. It's definitely one of the greatest things I've ever done."

Scott agreed, and added he hoped for more adventures in the future.

"For me, skiing from Jasper to Lake Louise at sixty-four was a confirmation that the adventures are not over," Scott said. "I've been lucky with hips and knees but I have also maintained my level of fitness all my life. It's not easy, but no one ever said that adventure was easy. And there are many good adventures yet to come."

A few hours after leaving the trailhead, our group crested the top of a round hill to look down into subalpine forest. With a clear blue sky, no wind and only a few puffy clouds drifting past rocky, snow-topped peaks, we decided to camp up high and enjoy the view.

It was indeed a sublime view, and to our delight the forecast storm did not arrive that night.

By morning, however, thick grey storm clouds were chugging toward us like an army of giant woolly caterpillars. We methodically dismantled our camp, repacking all the items that provided a reasonable amount of comfort for camping on snow, and settled under our packs once again. Although we'd each eaten a lunch, a dinner and a breakfast, the absence of that food did not lighten our loads quite as much as any of us might have hoped. Before long we'd descended from the firm, easy travelling surface of the high hills into a sugary, unconsolidated forest snowpack that caused us to repeatedly sink to our boot tops under the weight of our packs. With every metre descended the spaces between the trees tightened, making travel so laborious we almost didn't notice that the wind was whipping the tree tops back and forth as snowflakes began to flutter down from a darkening sky.

After more than a few acrobatic moves on skis with big packs swaying on our backs as we bushwhacked through tight willows and obstinate spruces, we reached an open valley bottom. Stopping for a snack and a drink, we realized the storm had arrived and completely swallowed the next high pass our route would head over. As we debated our options, Mike announced he didn't feel well. Steve, it turned out, thought he might have the flu, too.

Following a creekbed back to the north, we eventually merged onto a track-set cross-country ski trail which delivered us right back to the parking lot.

Our six-pass route had been reduced to one pass.

Maybe next year …

Best season: While a hiker could link a series of backcountry trails to cover the complete distance between Jasper and Lake Louise, the most direct – albeit most challenging – routes are possible in winter when snow covers swampy areas that are all but impassable in summer. For cross-country skiers of any level, there are more than 275 kilometres (170 miles) of trails in Jasper, many of them close to town. To rent equipment, visit www.jasperadventure-centre.com. For ski lessons, guided tours or information about the unique Maligne Canyon Icewalk, go to www.overlandertrekking.com. For snowshoe tours, visit www.walksntalks.com. For trail maps, stop in to the Parks Canada Information Centre in Jasper and pick up a free Winter Trails brochure.

Whistler Campground Loop, 4 kilometres (2.5 miles), easy, flat skiing, track-set for both classic and skate styles. Follow the Icefields Parkway south from Jasper for 2 kilometres (1.2 miles), turn right and then left to the campground entrance. If the gate is closed, there's not enough snow yet to ski.

Beaver Lake, 10 kilometres (6.2 miles), moderate hills, track-set for both classic and skate skiing. To access the start of this trail, drive east out of Jasper to the Highway 16 junction, then across the bridge onto Maligne Lake Road. Follow the road for 29 kilometres (18 miles) to the Beaver Creek picnic area, at the south end of Medicine Lake.

Shangri La Cabin, 8 kilometres (5 miles), 420 metres (1,378 feet), high point 2000 metres (6,562 feet).

This log cabin, built in 1936, was named after the imaginary Himalayan utopian kingdom of Shangri La described in James Hilton's very popular book *Lost Horizons*. Open December to April, the cabin is accessed by driving up Maligne Lake Road for about 40 kilometres (25 miles) to the unofficially named Rosemary's Rocks/Jeffreys Creek. Park in a plowed lot on the right, or if the river is not frozen, drive another kilometre and park in a lot on the left, just before a bridge. To book a night in this charming and very rustic log cabin, contact Bette Weir, Box 325

Jasper, Alberta, TOE 1E0. For detailed route descriptions, again check out Chic Scott's *Summits & Icefields*.

Six (Eight) Pass route, 50 kilometres (31 miles), 2170 metres (7,119 feet) elevation gain, high point 2475 metres (8,120 feet).

Most groups take four days to complete this classic Jasper backcountry ski traverse, camping for three nights along the way – there are no huts. See *Summits & Icefields*.

Skiing from Jasper to Banff via the east side of the Icefields Parkway is best begun from the Signal Mountain trailhead, accessed by driving east from Jasper to Maligne Lake Road, then up that road for 10 kilometres (6.2 miles). Topo maps *Athabasca Falls 83 C/12, Medicine Lake 83 C/13*.

For those with the necessary experience, skills, drive and stamina, the Great Divide Ski Traverse is one of the world's greatest backcountry skiing adventures, crossing glaciers and icefields and high alpine passes for about 300 kilometres (186 miles) for 20 to 30 days. You'll find full route info in *Summits & Icefields: Alpine Ski Tours in the Canadian Rockies*, by Chic Scott.

In summertime: Backpackers – or fit and fast trail runners – won't want to miss the Skyline trail, which reaches a maximum elevation of 2510 metres (8,235 feet) and stays there for 5 kilometres (3 miles), with sunny-day views clear to Mount Robson, the Canadian Rockies' highest peak, 80 kilometres (50 miles) to the north. Starting at Maligne Lake, 44 kilometres (27 miles) from the Highway 16 junction, this 44-kilometre (27-mile) backcountry trail is one of the true gems of Jasper National Park. You'll need to book ahead to score spots at the Little Shovel, Snowbowl, Curator or Tekarra campgrounds by calling 780.852.6176.

Hire a guide: If you don't have the requisite skills and experience, or you want to improve the skills you do have, hire a guide to take you on any of these adventures or to organize a custom trip: www.acmg.ca, www.yamnuska.com or www.internationalguidebureau.com.

Same Zen, Just Different

T he kayak I'm sitting in skims the lake surface so smoothly I feel like I'm moving through the calm water as if it's the most natural thing for me to do, as if I belonged there, butt-level with the water, as timeless as a fish.

But fish, I know, are not native to the Canadian Rockies' longest and largest naturally formed glacier-fed lake. Brook trout were the first to be introduced to Jasper's Maligne Lake in 1928, and later rainbow trout were added to the mix, the latter a dominant species that has thrived in the cold water. Fishers have been blissfully casting their lines into these gemstone turquoise waters ever since.

Note to self: someday, I must learn to fish.

For the moment, though, I'm paddling the length of the lake – all 22 kilometres (13.7 miles) of it – in a tandem sea kayak with sixteen-year-old Jonah in the aft seat, and his parents, Peter and Rochelle, each paddling their own kayaks a few boat-lengths away from us. We're bound for Coronet Creek campsite, on the lake's southernmost shore.

Gliding along on the smooth sheet of jade-toned liquid that's as glassy as mercury, I'm mesmerized by gentle ripples wafting across the surface like a silk sheet fluttering delicately in a soft breeze. The water is so green, so inviting to the eye, it reminds me of the Caribbean – but with the temperature of the Arctic.

Then, for a moment, the tranquility of my little world – which consists of the kayak that conceals my body from the waist down under a spray skirt, and carries a tent and three days' food for Jonah and myself inside watertight compartments fore and aft – is disturbed by the foreign sound of a motorboat.

The *Mary Schäffer* is named for the pre-eminent explorer who in 1908 embarked on a summer-long horseback expedition in search of a lake the Stoneys called Chaba Imne, or Beaver Lake. A Philadelphia Quaker with a keen interest in botany, Schäffer was the first non-Aboriginal woman to journey through the backcountry wilderness of much of what is now Jasper and Banff national parks. Upon reaching Maligne Lake, she realized it was the one railway surveyor Henry McLeod had named Sorefoot Lake in reference to the trials of his rough three-day journey from the Athabasca Valley. Over the next couple of decades a tote road was constructed linking the town of Jasper to Medicine Lake, from where travellers were ferried by boat to the lake's south shore to then ride horseback for the final leg of the journey to Maligne Lake. In 1927, Maligne Lake Chalet was built as part of outfitter Fred Brewster's Rocky Mountain Camps. Brewster's cluster of log buildings was, for a time, Jasper's most luxurious accommodation. In 1928, Rockies pioneer Donald "Curly" Phillips built the boathouse, which, now well stocked with modern rental canoes, is the last re-maining building of Curly's backcountry camp and one of few remaining structures of similar vintage in Alberta.

With those establishments, the era of private businesses op-erating in Canada's Rocky Mountain national parks was fully launched, and today's tour boat – one of more than a dozen that will pass us carrying loads of tourists during the three hours it takes us to paddle to the lake's midpoint, and the boats' turnaround point, Spirit Island – is testimony to the financial success of that private enterprise.

LOCALS' LORE: *A recognized National Historic Building, Maligne Lake Chalet was built in 1927, one of several log buildings, including the Guesthouse, the Cache and the Washhouse, all of which comprised outfitter Fred Brewster's backcountry lodge, operated by his Rocky Mountain Camp. A registered Alberta Historic Resource, the Curly Phillips Boathouse, built in 1928, is the last remaining building of the legendary guide and outfitter's Maligne Lake backcountry camp, and one of only a few structures in Alberta of similar vintage.*

Thankfully, each boat driver cuts his engine to avoid creating a wake so large it might tip our pod of three kayaks. Tour boat after tour boat, passengers line the deck railing to aim the cameras slung around their necks. I feel like a bighorn sheep on the side of the road.

"We are tourists, too," says Rochelle in response to a remark muttered by Jonah.

"No, we are travellers," Jonah insists. "Tourists take the tour boat."

Indeed we are travellers, and when the tour boat's motor has continued far enough down the lake that we can no longer hear it, I'm relieved to feel again like a traveller might have felt 100 years earlier.

The summer of 2011 marked the centennial of Mary Schäffer's second visit to Maligne Lake, when she journeyed back to Jasper on assignment for the Dominion government to survey and map the lake and its environs. After her trip, she made an application to the government to have a steam launch be operated on the lake. She also voiced her displeasure over a decision to exclude the lake and other areas from recently drawn national park boundaries. Her voice may have had an influence when the park boundaries later were redrawn and her beloved lake became protected from limitless development for future generations of wilderness lovers. One thing is for certain:

Same Zen

Rochelle O'Brien paddles calm water on Maligne Lake. Our group of four, including Rochelle's 16-year-old son, Jonah, camped for two nights at Coronet Creek campsite at the south end of the lake.

for all her travels by horseback train and log raft to explore Maligne's mysteries, Mary Schäffer never paddled its waters in a 21st-century durable plastic sea kayak.

After taking a break onshore at Spirit Island, we resume paddling down the lower half of the lake, gliding slowly past a succession of rough-hewn limestone walls and rocky turrets looming above us on all sides. As we put back into the water, I quickly realize how free and untethered I feel travelling this way. Skimming over the water, propelled only by our paddles, is quite unlike walking, skiing or riding a mountain bike or a horse: we leave behind only a ripple, even less than a footprint. As clouds close in, a breeze picks up, creating more ripples that leave the surface looking like a sheet of soft pewter after a violent hailstorm.

With my rain jacket hood keeping me comfortable through the shower, I realize that travelling by kayak does remind me of exploring the mountain wilderness by horseback, as its rhythmic pace provides time to think. And listen. With the tour boats long behind us, I hear birdsong. I hear the roar of Charlton Falls when they are still some distance downshore. We soon pass by the twin summits of mounts Charlton and Unwin, and I study their faces, trying to decipher the climbing route up Charlton's complicated, heavily crevassed glacier, knowing some of my friends climbed it last summer.

Hearing voices, we spot a couple paddling a canoe, moving steadily, yet slower than us. Although light, the wind forces me to push the paddle more forcefully to slice through the ripples, but I soon settle into the new rhythm comfortably enough to scan the surrounding lakeshore, every so often spying a small remnant glacier nestled between vertical cliff walls, no doubt a lot smaller than it was a century ago. I can't help but wonder how long those smaller glaciers might be around – twenty, fifty, a hundred years?

The wind picks up and a squall descends on us, spitting down a volley of graupel that plinks into the water, causing ephemeral vertical spikes to erupt from the surface. Then, as quickly as it sprang up, the squall abates, the waves settle down and more distant views become clearer. Looking at the north slopes of Mount Mary Vaux, I imagine shapes in giant patches of unmelted winter snow: a flat, spread-out map of Earth; a golden retriever's snout; a Dr. Seuss character.

I'm sightseeing, I decide, but seeing things very few people will ever see.

By the time we paddle into a small bay and pull up alongside a simple wooden boat dock, I'm acutely aware that my bare feet are cold in my damp sandals. Once out of the boat I root through the compartments to locate my gear bag. I've never been so happy to get into my hiking boots.

Soon we've erected our tents and boiled water for dinner, all the while under the watchful eye of a deer that shows little fear as it comes to within a few feet of our picnic table. Although we don't offer any food, it's obviously been fed before. When

A fisherman casts his line in the still water bathed in the golden light of dusk at the south end of Maligne Lake, Jasper National Park.

another deer joins him we decide to name them Chester and Wolfgang, and the following morning when we set off down the hiking trail that follows Coronet Creek farther south, Chester follows us like a lonely Labrador puppy for the entire first hour, until the trail emerges from the sheltered forest onto the gravel flats of the creek bed.

Slowly, Mount Mary Vaux slides into view to dominate the skyline behind us to the northwest, while up ahead Coronet Mountain glistens in the midday sun, its hanging glacier decorating the terraced cliff face like horizontal strips of meringue lining rock benches. Just out of view high above the east creek bank is the skyscraping summit of Mount Brazeau, at 3470 metres (11,385 feet), one of the Rockies' fifty-four 11,000ers. While the area had hosted numerous visitors for decades, the first ascent was not made until 1923 when Allen Carpe, Howard Palmer and outfitter William Harris muscled a sheet-iron boat with a mast and crude oars to the south end of Maligne Lake.

After a week of exploratory hiking they topped out on neighbouring Mount Henry Macleod and realized they were staring at Brazeau's "shapely crown" after having camped "at its base for a week without ever suspecting its identity."

Like them, I can't see Brazeau's glaciated flanks from Coronet Creek, but I still wonder how much that mountain has changed since their ascent. Gazing straight at Coronet's northwest hanging glacier, I notice some sculpted remnants of séracs pointed and dropping like expired party hats. The main section of glacier is creased with cracks, melting down smaller and smaller in the hot summer sun, before my eyes. Although we passed patches of snow in the shade of trees along the trail which we know was about 20 centimetres (8 inches) deep just two short days earlier, I also know it didn't snow enough last winter to help the Rockies glaciers grow. In fact, glaciologists conducting research on the Columbia Icefield, just 30 kilometres (18.6 miles) from here as the raven flies, discovered evidence of large-scale mid-winter melting that occurred during the endlessly sunny, warm days through last February and March.

I feel privileged to view the mountains as they are today, and can't help but wonder how many future generations might be able to do that.

Following the creek, the trail bumps up against a head-high dirt bank, leaving just a few rocks sticking out of the water for me to step on before I can hop across a narrow braid to regain the gravel trail. Grabbing a tree for support, I begin to move forward but stop in mid-swing. Lo and behold, there's a porcupine quietly taking a drink from the creek less than a metre (3 feet) from me. I stop dead and hold my breath as his needles bristle and he slowly climbs up the bank and partway up a tree just a few metres away, slowly enough that I have time to capture four quick photos.

The porcupine's slow, deliberate movements, like so many of the wondrous things in the mountains – the omnipresent rocks underfoot on the river flats, the countless spruce trees wallpapering the mountainsides, the puffy white clouds that drift across the sapphire sky, the brilliant fuchsia river beauties blooming where outlet creeks pour into the lake – are timeless, just like the beauty of this valley.

And we four are the only people here today.

The following morning we load up the kayaks for the trip home. Like so many of my backcountry trips, this one has to end far too soon. As I dip one blade of my paddle, then the other, into the tranquil morning water, the lake comes alive with the musical call of a loon. Before long the paddling feels Zen-like, not unlike the rhythm of skiing across a broad, flat glacier. Then suddenly we hit a patch of rough ripples and I laugh as I tuck my head into my hood and forge forward into the wind, realizing that this too feels a lot like skiing – into a headwind on the Wapta Icefield.

Same Zen, just different.

In an attempt to escape the wind and bouncy waves, we paddle close to the shore, where the water is unruffled, occasionally passing babbling creeks that we can hear before we see them. As soon as it hears us, a northern shoveller flushes from its hiding place among the shoreline grasses. Massive rocky peaks glide into view, one of them marked by a large rockfall scar that runs down a cliff face from a high ridge, the scar shaped like a giant arrowhead. It's mesmerizing to travel in the opposite direction and see a whole new view. Then, as we approach Spirit Island, I hear the first motorboat.

I'd completely forgotten about them.

Best season: Since the Maligne Lake region is sensitive wildlife habitat for a precariously small caribou herd, skiers are not encouraged to recreate here during the winter months. In summer, however, Maligne Lake provides an accessible starting point for countless mountain and water adventures.

Trailhead: From Jasper, drive east out of town to the Highway 16 junction and continue straight across the bridge to Moraine Lake Road. Follow the road for 44 kilometres (27.3 miles) and find a spot in the very large – and busy – parking lot. Topo maps *Athabasca Falls 83 C/12, Southesk Lake 83 C/11.*

Maligne Lake scenic cruise, 90 minutes on a comfortable motorboat. Don't forget your camera, as you'll be heading down the lake to internationally recognized Spirit Island. To book your trip, or even a private cruise, visit www.malignelake.com.

Have fun whitewater rafting on the Athabasca, Fraser or Sunwapta river, or try out an inflatable kayak: www.raftjasper.com.

Canoe, row or paddle a sea kayak on Maligne Lake. There's no better way to experience the lake than by paddling slowly on its aquamarine waters. Rentals are available at Curly Phillips Boathouse, www.malignelake.com. For information on campsites and safety tips for paddling on the lake, visit www.pc.gc.ca.

Paddle the whole length of Maligne Lake, 22 kilometres (13 miles) and camp at Coronet Creek Campground. If you've got the skills and experience, paddle about halfway down the lake and climb Mount Charlton, 3217 metres (10,554 feet), and Mount Unwin, 3268 metres (10,722 feet). See *Selected Alpine Climbs in the Canadian Rockies,* by Sean Dougherty. Alternatively, from the south end of the lake, keep on hiking up Coronet Creek and climb one of the Rockies' 11,000ers, Mount Brazeau, 3479 metres (11,414 feet), described in *The 11,000ers of the Canadian Rockies,* by Bill Corbett.

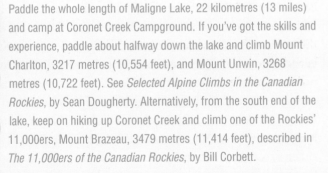

Hire a guide: If you don't have the requisite skills and experience to climb mounts Brazeau, Charlton or Unwin, hire a guide through www.acmg.ca, www.yamnuska.com or www.internationalguidebureau.com.

Y2Ski

The first snowmobiler to whiz by them didn't even register the presence of Karsten Heuer, Leanne Allison and Jay Honeyman as they skied steadily toward a tree-rimmed clearing at Kakwa Lake, BC, just beyond the northern tip of the Canadian Rockies.

After two weeks of skiing by day and camping in snow-blanketed wilderness under star-splattered skies by night, the trio emerged from the forest into a virtual outdoor showroom of motorized snow recreation vehicles. Midway through a 450-kilometre (280-mile), twenty-eight-day ski tour they'd launched two weeks earlier from Jasper, the trio was headed to Monkman Provincial Park, in northeastern BC.

The surprised snowmobilers, numbering more than 100, were gathered for an Easter weekend celebration. Exhibiting true northern hospitality toward the skiers, they generously shared moose steak sandwiches wrapped in white Wonder Bread slices. They would also end up being the only people Heuer, Allison and Honeyman would encounter during their entire ski tour.

The first people ever to ski the route, the three travelled for four weeks over remote and unspoiled Rockies slopes and valleys, following a course that was never less than three days' ski from the nearest plowed road.

More than a journey for its own sake, however, the ski tour would mark only the second leg of a 3400-kilometre (2,113-mile) journey for thirty-year-old Heuer, a Banff National Park warden and wildlife biologist. Starting out on June 16, 1998, from Yellowstone National Park in Wyoming, Heuer hiked, snowshoed, skied, canoed and bushwhacked for a total of 188 days in three separate sections, over several seasons and sometimes solo. His expedition concluded at Watson Lake, Yukon, on September 3, 1999. Dubbed the Y2Y Hike, Heuer's odyssey was a dedicated personal initiative aimed at increasing awareness of the Yellowstone to Yukon, or Y2Y, Conservation Initiative (www.y2y.net).

First conceived in 1993 by Calgary lawyer and conservationist Harvey Locke, Y2Y had grown, as of 2011, to encompass a network of more than 300 conservation organizations, wildlife scientists, agencies and First Nations groups working together at the grassroots in both Canada and the US to establish and maintain a system of core protected wildlife reserves linked together by wildlife movement corridors. The idea developed from growing scientific evidence that North America's current system of national parks, which forces animals into island-like protected areas, overlooks the fact that larger species such as wolves, wolverines and grizzlies require a much larger roaming area to avoid inbreeding and the challenges presented by natural disturbances such as fires, food shortages and disease. At a combined 20,238 square kilometres (7,814 square miles), the Canadian Rockies' Banff, Jasper, Yoho and Kootenay national parks comprise only one-sixth the area required to sustain 2,000 grizzly bears – the minimum number of individuals needed to maintain any one species.

(With an estimated 691 individuals remaining, the Alberta government finally, in June 2010, took the critical first step of declaring the grizzly a threatened species in that province. This was just a beginning, however. Much needs to be done to protect this species from human activities that fracture critical wildlife habitat – industrial development, forestry and oil and gas road networks, off-road recreation vehicles, rampant construction of vacation homes in towns such as Canmore, and high-speed traffic on the highways and railways, even inside Canada's national parks.)

When Heuer first learned of Y2Y in 1994, he wondered how possible it might actually be for an animal to travel the migration routes in their current state along the length of the Y2Y corridor. The question evolved into a quest, one that led Heuer to decide to travel the entire route himself, following one of several most likely large-mammal migration routes.

While resting his weary body after his summer 1998 journey, during which he had walked 2000 kilometres (1,200 miles) of rugged mountainous terrain from Yellowstone to Jasper over eighty-six days, Heuer spent much of the ensuing winter poring over maps, making phone calls and placing food caches. Travelling by ski, snowshoe and snowmobile, he made several forays into the backcountry to deliver his precious cache cargo, tightly secured in large steel paint cans clamped shut with wire levers to deter crafty four-legged scavengers.

Throughout his journey, friends, journalists and photographers joined Heuer for sections of his trek. But it was his childhood friend, Leanne Allison, who became his main partner, accompanying him for several weeks during the summer 1998 Yellowstone to Jasper segment, and again with third member Honeyman for the month-long ski tour. Then Allison signed on for the entire summer 1999 segment, which saw her, Heuer and Webster, his border collie, travelling through BC's largest roadless area, across uninhabited, rough terrain with few trails and numerous raging, unbridged rivers. On two separate occasions, the hikers were stalked by aggressive black bears, but they managed to carry on, physically unharmed, albeit unnerved.

Although the bears were sleeping during the ski portion of Heuer and Allison's journey, the winter leg presented its own challenges, as high alpine passes descended into dense valley-bottom bush during the final third of the ski traverse. For the last ten days their progress slowed from a steady 3 to 4 kilometres (2 to 2.5 miles) per hour to less than 1 kilometre (0.6 miles) per hour, as the thick, tangled forest forced the skiers to navigate by compass.

"We did things on skis I didn't know were even possible!" Allison exclaimed. An experienced mountaineer and back-country skier, she was no newcomer to adventure: in 1993 she was a member of the first all-woman team to climb the East Ridge of Canada's highest and notoriously challenging peak, 5959-metre (19,551-foot) Mount Logan.

"A lot of the terrain we crossed on skis is very wet and marshy, so it made more sense to travel it in winter," Heuer explained. "But winter is also a very interesting time to travel in terms of wildlife sign. You can see two or three days' worth in the snow."

While Heuer studied wildlife sign throughout his journey with the aim of learning more about how best to preserve the animals' natural habitat, when it came to route-finding through gorges blocked by vertical frozen waterfalls, it was the wildlife who repeatedly came to the humans' rescue.

"In some cases the wolverines showed us the best routes through canyon areas," Allison recalled.

Throughout the expedition, Heuer stopped along the way to visit communities in Wyoming, Montana, Alberta, British Columbia and Yukon to present talks and slide shows and share the Y2Y vision with the very people who live in these regions. To sometimes skeptical audiences, which included people who make their living from the land through forestry and mining and by operating remote hunting and fishing lodges, Heuer carefully explained how Y2Y hopes to draw up individual regional plans that include limited resource extraction and municipal growth plans, as well as tourism and recreation, all the while seeking ways in which wildlife and human populations can co-exist throughout the Rocky Mountains from the greater Yellowstone ecosystem all the way north to the Mackenzie Mountains in the Yukon.

By the end of his travels, Heuer says, he was pleased to find himself left with a feeling of optimism, since he had seen signs of grizzly bear or wolverine activity on all but thirty-one of the 188 days.

Fresh wolverine tracks show the telltale three-by-three-paw gait of one of the Rockies' most elusive and seldom seen inhabitants. When the Y2Y skiers route was blocked by seemingly impassable canyons, wolverine tracks often revealed the way through.

"As a biologist, when I first learned of Y2Y, I thought it was a pipe dream," he said. "But now, after covering the distance on foot, I'm pleased to learn that it is one small possible route already pretty much in place."

Perhaps ironically, one area with the most disturbance, Heuer learned, is the Bow Valley in the Alberta Rockies, which includes the towns of Banff and Canmore – and Heuer's own home and the Y2Y head office. With Banff situated in Banff National Park, and Canmore just outside the park's eastern boundary, human development in the region has created a bottleneck in a place where the natural geography of a narrow valley bordered by high, steep-walled mountains severely restricts mobility for animals.

For the Y2Y administrators, however, Heuer's efforts – which include a book, *Walking the Big Wild* – have been invaluable in raising awareness of Y2Y and about the reasons why such an initiative is necessary.

"Karsten has turned out to be a tremendously effective presenter as he talked to people about the fate of these great wilderness icons, like the grizzlies," said Bart Robinson, Y2Y network coordinator. "He's been so dedicated and committed to involving people and communities as he's moved across the landscape."

While for Heuer the journey, including the ski tour, was obviously a labour of passion, he admitted to experiencing a few wistful moments when he might have liked to lighten his purpose.

"We passed through incredible ski-touring terrain, passes that linked one beautiful bowl after another," he recalled. "It would have been nice to be able to take off our packs and make some turns."

AUTHOR'S NOTE: *Although I did not include the experience in this story – and it didn't make sense for Heuer to include it in* Walking the Big Wild *either – I was one of the journalists who accompanied him on part of his trek. Along with writer Mike Finkel* of Bozeman, Montana, I joined Heuer, Allison and Honeyman for the first four days of their ski-tour segment. Starting from Jasper in late March at the Decoigne warden cabin, we hoisted heavy multi-day packs (Finkel's and mine not nearly as large as the others' 70-pound/32-kilogram loads), we skied uphill and over flat meadows for a full day before pitching our camp in a sheltered, forested area not far from a running creek. That night, my first real winter camping experience was made much less daunting by Heuer's campfire talents.

Over the course of the two days it took us to reach the Miette warden cabin, we skied up a broad trail through spruce forest, wove our way up a partially frozen waterfall on steep and narrow snow ledges, and stopped to admire the luge-like paths created by pine martens as they slid down pillowy snow slopes to plunge under the snow-cover into running creek water. It was, for me, at the time a novice backcountry skier unaccustomed to carrying a big pack, a physically challenging trip. Although I didn't know it at the time, such trips would become easier as I continued to make them, but one thing I did know was that such a trip was indeed my idea of heaven.

After two nights at the primitive warden cabin, during which time Allison's blisters healed, a snowstorm abated and much laughter was shared, I watched wistfully as Allison, Heuer and Honeyman skied off early in the morning, climbing smoothly up a powdery slope carrying all the gear they'd need to stay alive in the remote Rockies landscape. Then they dropped over the top of the pass and out of sight. It took Finkel and me a full ten hours to ski back to the road that day, and I reached the parking lot feeling sore but energetic, inspired and alive.

Best seasons: To the best of anyone's knowledge, Karsten Heuer is the only person – certainly in modern times – to have hiked, skied, canoed and snow-shoed the entire 3400 kilometres (2,113 miles) from Yellowstone to the Yukon following the spine of the Rockies. And certainly the 450-kilometre (280-mile) segment between Jasper and Monkman Provincial Park in northeastern BC is best explored in winter to avoid extensive marshy areas. Hiking the Great Divide Trail, which covers 1200 kilometres (746 miles) from Waterton Lakes National Park to Kakwa Lake Provincial Park in BC, can be comfortably completed over two months, or a good chunk of the Rockies summer season. For full route info, pick up *Hiking Canada's Great Divide Trail*, by Dustin Lynx. And while keen backcountry skiers will appreciate the unparalleled solitude of visiting the Robson area in winter, this is without doubt one of the Rockies' premier summer hiking destinations.

Trailhead: For your own adventure in the Rockies north of Jasper, follow Highway 16 to Mount Robson Provincial Park, home of the highest peak in the Canadian Rockies, 3954-metre (12,972-foot) Mount Robson. Topo map *Mount Robson 83 E/3.*

Kinney Lake, 4.2 kilometres (2.6 miles), 120 metres (394 feet) elevation gain, high point 975 metres (3200 feet).

Even before you reach Kinney Lake, which is an absolutely captivating shade of turquoise found only in glacier-fed lakes, the trail from the parking lot is lined with a rare sight in the Rockies – a micro-rainforest of Douglas fir, spruce, hemlock and massive old-growth cedar. This ecological pocket is the product of abundant rainfall deposited in the valley when Pacific weather systems collide with Robson's immense bulk.

Whitehorn Campground backpack, 10.5 kilometres (6.5 miles), 273 metres (896 feet) elevation gain, high point 1128 metres (3,700 feet).

For a delightful backpacking destination without too much work, Whitehorn campground offers a tranquil resting spot, complete with spacious cook shelter, after a bit of a stiff climb. Give yourself a couple of nights so you can hike up – and it *is* uphill! – to Berg Lake the next day without the weight of your backpack.

Berg Lake Campground, 19.6 kilometres (12 miles), 795 metres (2,608 feet) elevation gain, high point 1652 metres (5,420 feet).

Berg Lake is, hands-down, one of my top five places to camp in the Rockies. Listen as chunks of Berg Glacier break off and splash into the lake, then wait a few minutes to hear waves lap onto the beach on the opposite shore, where the campsite is located. Give yourself a few days and hike to Toboggan Falls and Snowbird Pass. See *The Canadian Rockies Trail Guide*, by Brian Patton and Bart Robinson.

Bust a Lung!

Mount Robson, 3954 metres (12,972 feet), Northeast Face/Southeast Ridge IV.

On average, only 15 per cent of parties aiming to stand on this monstrous Rockies summit succeed in any given season, and for very good reason. It has a Himalayan-scale, 3000-metre (9,843-foot) base-to-summit rise with big, complicated terrain, frequent deteriorations in conditions, and notoriously nasty weather – all of which combine to make any ascent of Robson by its half-dozen established lines a very serious undertaking. US alpinist Steve House once presented a 90-minute slide show describing his multiple attempts – and failures – to climb the "King." For full route info, see *The 11,000ers of the Canadian Rockies*, by Bill Corbett.

Hire a guide: If you don't have the requisite skills and experience, hire a guide to take you on any of these adventures or to organize a custom trip: www.acmg.ca, www.yamnuska.com or www.internationalguidebureau.com.

LOCALS' LORE: *Believe it or not, a very few extraordinary ski mountaineers have skied Mount Robson. In summer 1983, BC-based filmmaker/adventurer Peter Chrzanowski skied down its ridiculously exposed Southeast Ridge, in places a mere 10 metres (33 feet) wide. Then, in September 1995, BC ski mountaineers Troy Jungen and Ptor Spricenieks snagged one of North America's plum extreme descents when they skied from the summit down Robson's 1000-metre (3,280-foot) North Face.*

Reference Books

The following guidebooks contain detailed information about many of the adventures described in this book, plus a whole lot more!

Corbett, Bill. *The 11,000ers of the Canadian Rockies*. Calgary: Rocky Mountain Books, 2004.

Daffern, Gillean. *Kananaskis Country Trail Guide Volume 1: Kananaskis Valley, Kananaskis Lakes, Elk Lakes, The Smith-Dorrien*. Calgary: Rocky Mountain Books, 2010.

Dettling, Peter. *The Will of the Land*. Calgary: Rocky Mountain Books, 2010.

Dougherty, Sean. *Selected Alpine Climbs in the Canadian Rockies*. Calgary: Rocky Mountain Books, 1999.

Eastcott, Doug. *Backcountry Biking in the Canadian Rockies*. Calgary: Rocky Mountain Books, 1999.

Fisher, Chris, Don Pattie and Tamara Hartson. *Mammals of the Rocky Mountains*. Edmonton: Lone Pine Publishing, 2000.

Gadd, Ben. *Handbook of the Canadian Rockies*. Jasper: Corax Press, 2004.

Haberl, Keith, and Tami Knight. *Alpine Huts: A Guide to the Facilities of the Alpine Club of Canada*. Canmore: Alpine Club of Canada, 1995.

Heuer, Karsten. *Walking the Big Wild: Yellowstone to Yukon on the Grizzly Bear Trail*. Toronto: McClelland & Stewart, 2002.

Isaac, Sean. *Mixed Climbs in the Canadian Rockies*. 2nd ed. Calgary: Rocky Mountain Books, 2004.

Josephson, Joe. *Waterfall Ice: Climbs in the Canadian Rockies*. 4th ed. Calgary: Rocky Mountain Books, 2002.

Kane, Alan. *Scrambles in the Canadian Rockies*. New ed. Calgary: Rocky Mountain Books, 2006.

Kershaw, Linda, Andy MacKinnon and Jim Pojar. *Plants of the Rocky Mountains*. Edmonton: Lone Pine Publishing, 1998.

Lynx, Dustin. *Hiking Canada's Great Divide Trail*. Calgary: Rocky Mountain Books, 2007.

Oltmann, Ruth. *My Valley: The Kananaskis*. Calgary: Rocky Mountain Books, 1997.

Patton, Brian, and Bart Robinson. *The Canadian Rockies Trail Guide: A Hiker's Guide to Banff, Jasper, Yoho, Kootenay, Waterton Lakes, Mount Robson, Mount Assiniboine, Peter Lougheed, Elk Lakes and Akamina–Kishinena Parks*. 8th ed. Banff: Summerthought Publishing, 2007.

Perry, Chris, and Joe Josephson. *Bow Valley Rock*. Calgary: Rocky Mountain Books, 2000.

Potter, Mike. Central Rockies Wildflowers. Banff: Luminous Compositions, 1996.

Rollins, Jon. *Caves of the Canadian Rockies and the Columbia Mountains*. Calgary: Rocky Mountain Books, 2004.

Sanford, Emerson, and Janice Sanford Beck. *Life of the Trail* series, 6 vols. Calgary: Rocky Mountain Books, 2008, 2009, 2010, 2011.

Scott, Chic. *Deep Powder and Steep Rock: The Life of Mountain Guide Hans Gmoser*. Banff: Assiniboine Publishing, 2009.

_____. *Powder Pioneers*. Calgary: Rocky Mountain Books, 2005.

_____. *Pushing the Limits*. Calgary: Rocky Mountain Books, 2000.

_____. *Ski Trails in the Canadian Rockies*. Calgary: Rocky Mountain Books, 2005.

_____. *Summits & Icefields: Alpine Ski Tours in the Canadian Rockies*. New ed. Calgary: Rocky Mountain Books, 2008.

Scott, Chic, Ben Gadd and Dave Dornian. *The Yam: 50 Years of Climbing on Yamnuska*. Calgary: Rocky Mountain Books, 2003.

Scott, Jim. *Backcountry Huts & Lodges of the Rockies & Columbias*. Calgary: Johnson Gorman, 2001.

Glossary

ACMG. Association of Canadian Mountain Guides, formed in 1963; first non-European member of the International Federation of Mountain Guides Associations, the worldwide body which oversees professional mountain guiding.

alpine. The mountain region above treeline; climbing activities undertaken in this region.

alpinist. A climber who seeks aesthetic and often difficult routes in the alpine region rather than the easiest path to a summit.

anchor. A point where several pieces of climbing gear are placed in the rock to secure the rope, from which the leader belays their partner (the seconder) up to them or climbers may descend by rappelling (*see* **rappel**). Sturdy tree trunks and immovable rock features can also be used.

belay. The act of managing a climbing rope using friction to ensure the climber will not fall far should they slip (*see also* **protection**); **belayer**: the person belaying the climber.

bergschrund. A crevasse that forms where gravity causes glacier ice to pull away from the mountainside, usually near the upper section of the glacier.

bivy. Short for the French term "bivouac," an impromptu camp on the side of a mountain, usually with minimal or no camping gear.

bonk. Expression used by outdoor sports enthusiasts to denote exercise-induced low blood sugar, which causes a feeling of light-headedness and weakness in all limbs.

cairn. A man-made stone pile built as a trail marker or to mark a summit.

carabiner. A metal loop with a hinged gate through which a rope is passed, and which is hooked onto another piece of climbing gear that is in turn attached to the mountain. *See also* **anchor**, **belay**, **gear**, **piton**, **protection**.

cat-skiing. Downhill skiing that takes place in remote backcountry wilderness using a snowcat – an enclosed, heated, truck-sized cab equipped with bulldozer-style tracks designed to travel easily on snow.

chimney. An enclosed section on a rock wall that has two or three sides close enough together that climbers, using their hands and feet, can apply opposing pressure to the front, back and side walls to inch themselves upward.

chossy. Poor-quality, crumbly rock.

climber. A person who climbs mountains via steep rock, snow or ice routes, not necessarily to reach a summit.

committing. A move which, once undertaken, cannot be easily or safely reversed.

cornice. A wind-blown shelf of snow that hangs suspended in mid-air beyond a mountain ridge.

crevasse. A crack or fissure on a glacier surface, often found in places where the glacier bed pulls the ice sheet more steeply downhill. Crevasses can be hundreds of metres deep.

exposure. In climbing, the amount of air, or space, between the climber and the ground below. An unprotected (that is, unroped and with no gear or means of securing the climber to the mountain) fall in an exposed place would almost guarantee death.

gear. Climbing hardware, camming devices, metal nuts and pins placed into the rock to which a carabiner is attached and the rope threaded through in order to minimize the distance a climber will fall in case of a slip. *See also* **anchor, belay, carabiner, piton, protection**.

glacier. A large mass of ice formed by multiple layers of snow compacted under its own weight which eventually forms a sheet with sufficient mass to slide downhill.

graupel. Soft hail or snow pellets.

heli-ski. Downhill skiing in wilderness areas where a helicopter is used to ferry skiers to the top of a run, from where they ski downhill to a pickup point to repeat the shuttle.

icefall. The part of a glacier that has been pulled down a steep section under its own weight, and which is broken and fractured by numerous crevasses.

icefield. An extensive mass of glacial ice which may feed many glaciers flowing downward from its edges.

krummholz. Stunted, twisted trees found in the subalpine, or the highest reaches of the treeline region.

mountaineer. One who climbs for sport, usually aiming to reach a summit via a route of easy to moderate difficulty via a mix of rock, snow and glacial features.

névé. Partially compacted granular snow that forms the upper part of a glacier.

pitch. A rope length on a steep climb. Anchors are built at the top of each pitch. *See also* **anchor, belay, carabiner, gear, piton, protection**.

piton. A metal spike with an eye drilled in one end through which a carabiner and rope can be secured; the spike is hammered into a crack in the rock.

protection. Process of setting equipment or anchors for safety; equipment or anchors used for arresting falls; commonly known as "pro."

rappel. To lower oneself on a rope threaded through an anchor. *See also* **anchor, belay, protection**.

scree. Loose, broken rock debris that litters many mountain slopes.

sérac. A column, pinnacle or sharp block of ice amidst crevasses on a glacier.

skins. Textured synthetic strips that are applied to ski bases for walking uphill, which slide smoothly over the snow in a forward direction but prevent backward sliding. They are removed to allow for downhill skiing.

ski touring. Ascending mountain slopes by walking uphill on skis using skins, without mechanized lifts, and then skiing downhill. Special ski bindings release at the heel to facilitate the climbing motion, then are reattached for downhill skiing.

solo. To climb alone, often without a rope.

spindrift. Fine, loose snow particles transported by wind.

splitboard. A snowboard that separates into two halves for climbing up slopes using skins (*see* **skins**), then reattaches to be ridden like a regular snowboard for descending.

sport climbing. Rock climbing on steep routes that have been fitted with bolts permanently drilled into the rock to which the rope is attached to facilitate very safe climbing.

talus. A sloping mass of rock debris at the base of a cliff.

technical climbing. Climbing that requires a rope for protection to be navigated safely.

telemark. A specialized ski technique which employs boots that hinge at the binding toe piece, with the heel remaining free to move up and down. Telemark was the original downhill ski technique.

traditional climbing. Rock climbing on steep cliffs and walls where there are no permanent bolts, requiring climbers to place removable metal nuts and camming devices attaching the rope.

treeline. The upper limit at which trees grow on a mountainside.

verglas. A thin, nearly transparent layer of ice coating the rocks on a mountain.

yo-yo skiing. To climb and descend the same mountain slope repeatedly.

Acknowledgements

Thanks to everyone who has written down passages of Canadian Rockies history and adventure before me, so I might learn their tales and interpret them through my own Rockies experiences, especially:

Jerry Auld
Bill Corbett
Tony and Gillean Daffern
Peter Dettling
Dave Dornian
Bruno Engler
Ben Gadd
Keith Haberl
Karsten Heuer
Joe Josephson
Sid Marty
Ruth Oltmann
Brian Patton
Carol Picard
Bart Robinson
Bob Sandford
Emerson Sanford
Janice Sanford Beck
Chic Scott
Cindy Smith
Jon Whyte

Special thanks to Suzan Chamney and Pat Morrow for their valuable advice, and to Chyla Cardinal for her patience, enthusiasm and layout wizardry skills that brought this book to life! Many mountains of thanks also to my terrific adventure partners and my totally amazing family.

Index